Beautiful Borders & Backings & Bindings

by Jill Reber and Margaret Sindelar

Landauer Books

Beautiful Borders & Backings Bindings

Copyright © 2005 By Landauer Corporation
Projects copyright © 2004 By Jill Reber and Margaret Sindelar

This book was designed and produced by Landauer Books.
A division of Landauer Corporation
3100 NW 101st Street, Suite A
Urbandale, Iowa 50322
www.landauercorp.com 800/557-2144

President and Publisher: Jeramy Lanigan Landauer
Director of Operations: Kitty Jacobson
Editor-in-Chief: Becky Johnston
Art Director: Linda L. Bender
Technical Editor: Eve Mahr
Photographers: Craig Anderson, Dennis Kennedy

Printed in China

ISBN 13: 978-1-890621-81-0

10 9 8 7 6 5 4

Library of Congress Cataloging-in-Publication Data

Reber, Jill.
    Beautiful borders, backings & bindings: a step-by-step illustrated guide to fabulous finishing techniques featured in 10 easy projects / by Jill Reber and Margaret Sindelar.
        p. cm.
    ISBN 1-890621-81-1
1. Quilting. 2. Borders, Ornamental (Decorative arts) I. Sindelar, Margaret, 1945- II. Title.
TT835.R383 2004
746.46--dc22
                                    2004057629

About the Authors

Jill Reber, is a prolific quilter who has made more that 150 quilts in the past 15 years, many of which are featured in this book. As a pattern designer, teacher, and seminar leader, she travels extensively sharing her personal techniques. Jill and her husband are the creators of Master Piece® Rulers, Static Stickers template material, and companion quilting products. Contact Jill at Master Piece® Products, 10481 NW 107th Ave., Granger, IA 50109.

Margaret Sindelar's remarkable career spans more than 30 years as a needlework teacher, professional designer and photo stylist for leading magazine and book publishers including *Better Homes and Gardens*, *McCall's Quilting*, *That Patchwork Place*, and *Landauer Books*. Margaret creates works of enduring art through her design company Cottonwood Classics. Margaret is the author of *Making Memories*. Margaret can be reached at Cottonwood Classics, 4813 Cody Drive, West Des Moines, IA 50265.

Contents

Introduction

To help you choose the perfect finish and complete your quilted creations with confidence, co-authors and designers, Jill Reber and Margaret Sindelar combine their expertise from years of professional quilting and designing in this comprehensive 144-page needle arts technique book.

Browse through the galleries of new and antique quilt borders, backings, and bindings. Select from the myriad of choices and practice projects to help you master the ABC's of everything from appliqué to borders with curves. You'll find it all here with helpful tips along the way—

- cutting parallelograms (commonly referred to as *diamonds)* for shape and movement
- using *triangles* to repeat a patchwork design
- creating *appliqué* borders for dimension
- adding depth with plaids, stripes or bold prints using *mitered* corners
- borrowing *irregular borders* from an antique quilt
- placing *simple blocks* for an all-around frame or corner complements
- bordering with *rectangles* used as piano keys, to repeat color values or even to introduce fabrics for a new color palette
- featuring gentle *curves and scallops* for a graceful finish
- keeping it simple with *squares*
- learning the techniques for most-often-used *bindings*
- trying distinctive *edgings* with step-by-step photos to guide you

To learn six classic border treatments including appliqué, choose the impressive quilt *Working My Way Around,* or start small with projects ranging from wallhangings to table toppers. Clearly written, easy-to-understand, illustrated in full-color with complete instructions, diagrams and step-by-step photos, this book will be one of the most useful reference books in your quilting library.

Piecing the patchwork top is only the beginning. Adding the perfect border, backing, and binding to complete the quilt will make it uniquely yours—from start to finish!

Becky Johnston, Editor-in-Chief

Borders

Discover how adding a border to a quilt top not only increases the size, but enhances the carefully crafted center so that it becomes the frame on a personalized work of art. To help you choose the perfect border for your quilt, we've created a gallery of border ideas for your inspiration.

To learn six classic border treatments including the art of appliqué, choose an impressive quilt *Working My Way Around*, or start small with projects ranging from wallhangings to table toppers. You'll find it all on the following pages with helpful tips along the way.

borders with
DIAMONDS

For a visual adventure, try your hand at borders with parallelograms, commonly referred to as diamonds—on point, in rows, floating on a background or in sawtooth edges—they provide unlimited possibilities for adding color, shape, and movement to any quilt border.

borders with
TRIANGLES

The angular geometry of triangles provides the opportunity to build a natural fence, repeat patchwork designs from a quilt center, or create a sense of undulating motion around the edge of almost any border.

borders with
APPLIQUÉ

From the delicate details of birds, flowers and
flowing vines to the crisp points of geometric
snowflakes and stars, appliqué borders add
dimension, movement, and visual interest to
plain or pieced borders.

borders with
MITERED CORNERS

Plaids, stripes, and bold prints all lend themselves to mitering. With careful planning this right-angle finish creates a new design motif, moves the eye around the quilt, and frames the quilt with the illusion of depth.

borders with
IRREGULAR
EDGES

The irregularly shaped edges of scrappy antique quilts add visual interest and soften the lines of patchwork—often making the border the unexpected focal point of the quilt.

24

borders with
CORNER
BLOCKS

Placing corner blocks in borders anchors and complements the design elements in a quilt top. Blocks that are a repeat from the quilt center are a natural choice. If size is a consideration, use a small square or half-square triangle for the corner block. Blocks that continue around the corner of a quilt top reinforce design and symmetry—and an entire border of quilt blocks creates a visual frame.

borders with
RECTANGLES

For a quick-to-cut border treatment, try a wide array of
rectangles arranged as if paving with bricks, fencing
the forest, or lining up the keys on a piano. Fabric
scraps from the quilt center are often used to repeat
the colors and values, but for contrast experiment with
introducing fabrics in a new color palette to accent
the quilt center.

borders with
CURVES
&ROUNDED
CORNERS

Patiently pieced arched blocks like Double
Wedding Ring and Apple Core deserve
special treatment. To soften the edges of a
quilt, gentle curves and scallops featured as
the final border are the graceful answer.

30

borders with
SQUARES

Squares are often a natural choice for borders—they are easy to cut and quick to assemble—offering almost instant results for quilters on the go. For greater impact, try arranging small squares in a checkerboard for the corner blocks. Repeat fabric from the quilt center or choose complementary fabrics to march a line of squares on point row by row around the edge of the quilt top.

Border Projects

If you're searching for a project to help you master the ABC's of everything from appliqué to borders with curved corners and diamonds on the diagonal, dive into the delightful projects featured on the following pages. All of the projects designed by Jill or Margaret include complete instructions with step-by-step illustrated how-to's and full-size patterns. From large to small, you're sure to find a quilted project with beautiful borders that's perfect to keep or to give as a gift.

Border Projects

WORKING MY WAY AROUND
Page 36

*Practice border techniques by sewing a simple border sampler.
Working My Way Around features six borders surrounding a
center of star blocks that could stand alone as a small wallhanging.*

PINEAPPLE PLEASURES
Page 56

*A cheerful table runner inspired by a yellow-and-white print
featuring pineapples offers three beautiful borders—pineapple,
sawtooth, and rectangles with corner squares.*

VINE AND FLOWERS
Page 60

*Learn two useful border techniques from this eye-catching project!
Master mitered corners to enhance striped borders—even when the
stripes are subtle. Then practice your appliqué skills on a gracefully
curved vine and colorful flowers.*

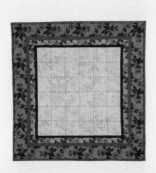

VENETIAN STEPS
GARDEN'S GLORY
Page 68

*Boldly striped fabrics beg to be mitered, sometimes with
surprising results. Can't find a stripe that suits you? Learn
how to make your own from suitable purchased fabrics.*

STRAWBERRIES & CREAM
Page 70

Double-frame a bold scenic print with a simple border surrounded by graceful scallops while you learn the technique of clean-finish edges.

WEATHERVANE STAR
Page 74

For a little night music add a piano-key border to a winter warmer featuring a weathervane star. This scrappy quilt with corner blocks on the border is a stash-keeper's delight.

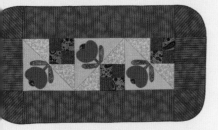

ORANGE BLOSSOM
Page 78

Bring blooms and blossoms to your table on a table runner that features simple appliqué and patchwork, plus easy-to-make curved corner blocks.

GLORIFIED NINE PATCH
Page 82

It's easy to visualize these interlocking circles, adapted from an antique quilt, extending all the way around a simple quilt. To help you master the graceful curved edges, we've included full-size patterns and some special helps.

CHECKERBOARD STAR
Page 89

There's plenty of block and border interest in this patchwork table topper. Best of all, these stripes and checks are so easy to make you'll want to use the technique often.

Practice border techniques by sewing a simple border sampler. Working My Way Around *features six borders surrounding a center of star blocks that could stand alone as a small wallhanging.*

WORKING MY WAY AROUND

Quilt   By Jill Reber

MATERIALS

2 yards floral fabric for center stars, diamond
border corners and outside border

•

5 yards backing fabric

•

¾ yard dark green print for binding

•

Batting to fit finished quilt top

Approximate finished size: 78"x78"

*The yardages given here are for the
floral outer border fabric used in
two additional borders plus the
finishing materials. Yardages for
each border are included with the
instructions for the projects
featured on the following pages.*

MATERIALS FOR EACH BORDER

BORDER ONE–FLYING GEESE

⅓ yard red print
for border frames
•
⅓ yard tan for background
•
5¼"x42" strips of
4 assorted red prints for
Flying Geese

BORDER TWO–SQUARES ON POINT

3⅜"x42" strip of
4 different medium purple
prints for squares
•
½ yard tan for background

BORDER THREE–RAMBLING VINE

1 yard tan for background
•
½ yard dark green solid
for vine
•
Assorted scraps of green
prints for leaves

BORDER FOUR–SQUARES IN A ROW

3½"x42" strips of 6
assorted medium red prints
•
3½"x42" strips of
6 assorted dark red prints

BORDER FIVE–DIAMONDS WITH DIRECTION

3½"x42" strips of 8
assorted dark purple prints
for diamonds
•
1⅛ yards tan for
background
•
2⅜"x42" strip dark green
solid for star points
•
4—3½" squares floral
border print

BORDER SIX–BASIC WRAP BORDER

Remaining floral print

MATERIALS

•

¼ yard tan for background

•

2⅞"x42" strips of 2 different dark green prints
for star points

•

4½"x42" strip of floral print for star centers

*Finished size: 16½" square
including seam allowances*

Cutting

From tan background,
  Cut 1— 2½"x42" strip. Cut into 16—2½" squares.
• Cut 4—5¼" squares. Cut in half diagonally twice, for
    16 quarter-square triangles.

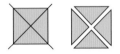

From each dark green print strip,
• Cut 8—2⅞" squares. Cut in half once diagonally for
    16 half-square triangles.

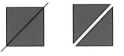

From floral print,
• Cut 4—4½" squares.

QUILT CENTER
Stars

Assembling

Use a ¼" seam allowance for all seams.

1. Sew 2 green half-square triangles to each tan background
   triangle, as shown, to make a Flying Geese unit. Make 16.
   Press seams towards small triangles.

2. For each block, arrange 4 Flying Geese, 4 tan squares and
   a floral square in rows as shown. Sew the pieces into rows.
   Sew the rows together. Make 4.

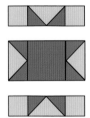

3. Sew the 4 blocks together as shown.

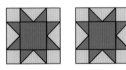
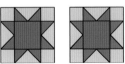
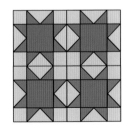

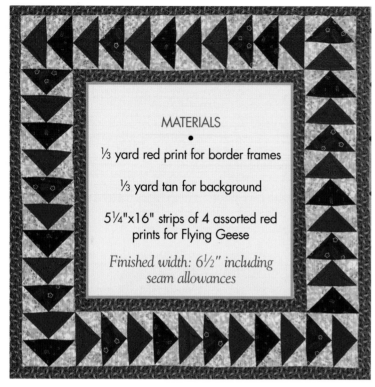

BORDER ONE
Flying Geese

Flying Geese Units

Cutting

From each of 4 assorted red prints,
• Cut 3—5¼" squares. Cut in half diagonally twice for 12 quarter-square triangles. (You will only use 11 quarter-square triangles of each fabric.)

From tan background,
• Cut 4—2⅞"x42" strips. Cut into 44—2⅞" squares, cut in half diagonally once for 88 half-square triangles.

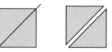

Assembling

Use a ¼" seam allowance for all seams.

1. Sew 2 tan half-square triangles to each red print triangle as shown, to make a Flying Geese unit. Make 44. Press seams towards small triangles.

Inside Border Frame

Cutting

From red border-frame print,
• Cut 2—1½"x16½" rectangles
• Cut 2—1½"x18½" rectangles

Assembling

Use a ¼" seam allowance for all seams.

1. Sew the 2—1½"x16½" rectangles to the top and bottom of the quilt top. Press seams towards the border.
2. Sew the 2—1½"x18½" rectangles to the sides of the quilt top. Press seams towards the border.

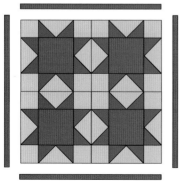

2. Sew 9 Flying Geese units together as shown. Repeat to make 2. Sew to top and bottom of the quilt top.

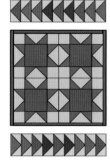

3. Sew 13 Flying Geese together as shown. Notice that the two geese left are going a different direction. Repeat to make 2.

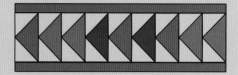

Sew to sides of the quilt top.

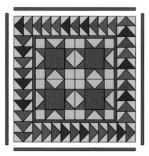

Outside Border Frame

Cutting

From red border-frame print,
• Cut 2—1½"x26½" rectangles
• Cut 2—1½"x28½"rectangles

Assembling

Use a ¼" seam allowance for all seams.

1. Sew the 2—1½"x26½" rectangles to the top and bottom of the quilt top. Press seams towards the border.
2. Sew the 2—1½"x28½" rectangles to the sides of the quilt top. Press seams towards the border.

Use one or more border frames to dramatize a pieced border. Insert a framing border to adjust a quilt top and make it fit a specific sized pieced border.

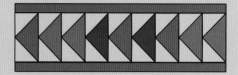

Draw extra attention to an interesting border by framing with small Flying Geese surrounding it.

Directional borders like Flying Geese add a sense of motion around the edge of a quilt.

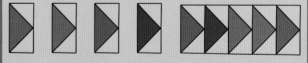

Achieve a completely different look by reversing the darks and lights of a Flying Geese border.

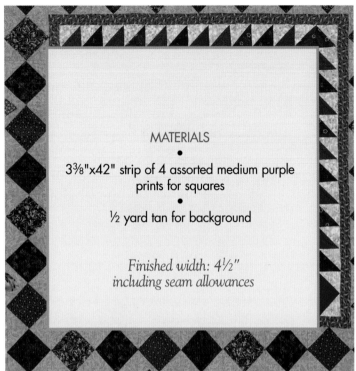

BORDER TWO
Squares on Point

Cutting

From each medium purple print strip,
• Cut 8—3⅜" squares for a total of 32 squares

From background tan,
• Cut 5—2⅞"x42" strips. Cut into 64—2⅞" squares. Cut in half diagonally once for 128 half-square triangles.

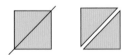

MATERIALS

•

3⅜"x42" strip of 4 assorted medium purple prints for squares

•

½ yard tan for background

Finished width: 4½"
including seam allowances

Assembling

Use a ¼" seam allowance for all seams.

1. Sew tan background triangles to opposite sides of the medium purple squares as shown. Repeat for remaining sides as shown. Unit should measure 4½" including seam allowances. Make 32.

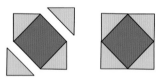

2. Sew 7 units together as shown. Repeat to make two strips. Sew to top and bottom of quilt top. Press toward quilt top.

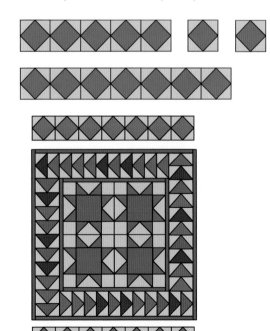

3. Sew 9 units together as shown. Repeat to make two strips. Sew to sides of quilt top. Press toward quilt top.

TIPS
FOR BETTER BORDERS

Make sure your seam allowances are precise so your corners stay square. There should be a ¼" seam allowance beyond the square points.

Use a light background fabric for the small triangles and the Squares On Point appear to float around your quilt.

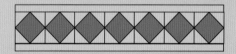

Reverse the lights and darks to achieve a different look. Alternate squares of an assortment of fabrics from the quilt center to emphasize the center.

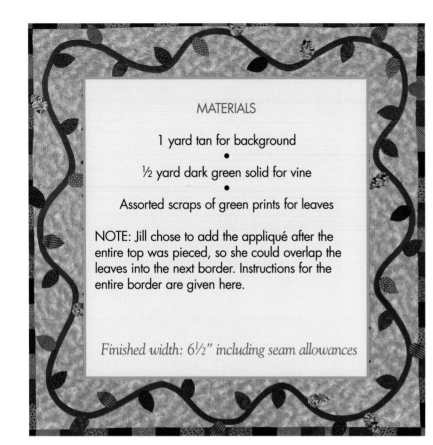

MATERIALS

1 yard tan for background

•

½ yard dark green solid for vine

•

Assorted scraps of green prints for leaves

NOTE: Jill chose to add the appliqué after the entire top was pieced, so she could overlap the leaves into the next border. Instructions for the entire border are given here.

Finished width: 6½" including seam allowances

BORDER THREE
Rambling Vine

Background Border

Cutting

From the background tan,
• Cut 2—6½"x36½" strips
• Cut 3—6½"x42" strips

Assembling

Use a ¼" seam allowance for all seams.

1. Sew the 6½"x36½" rectangles to the top and bottom of the quilt top. Press seams toward tan fabric.

2. Cut one 6½"x42" strip into 2—6½"x21" strips. Sew strips together and trim to make 2— 6½"x48½" rectangles. Sew the 6½"x48½" rectangles to the sides of the quilt top.

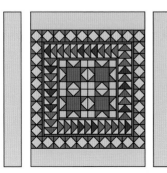

Vine

Assembling

1. Cut a 45-degree angle on one edge of the ½-yard piece of dark green solid. Cut 9—2" bias strips as shown. (See Bias Strips, right.)

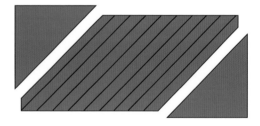

2. Sew the strips together to make one long bias strip.

3. Fold the strip lengthwise into thirds and press.

4. Arrange the bias strip on the background border in a curving vine shape. Refer to Glossary of Terms (page 133) for hand or machine appliqué.

BIAS STRIPS

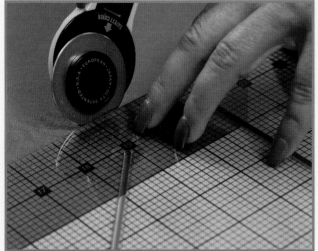

1. Cut 9—2" bias strips from the ½ yard of green solid, as shown.

4. Press seams to one side.

2. Seam the strips together forming one long bias strip.

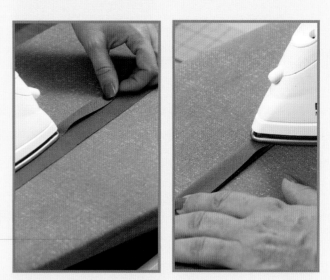

5. Fold and press the bias into thirds to form a finished vine.

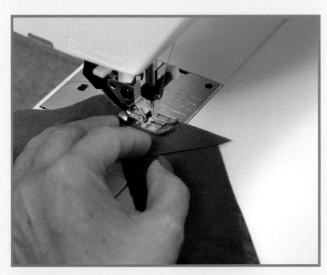

3. Handle carefully to avoid stretching the bias.

6. Draw or free form a pleasing vine within the border space. Baste or pin in place.

TEMPLATE APPLIQUÉ

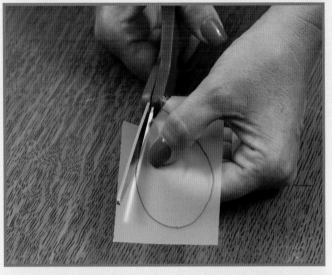

1. Trace the Leaf pattern onto template plastic. Cut out with paper scissors.

3. Cut out leaves allowing a ¼" seam allowance to extend beyond the drawn line.

2. Trace around template with an erasable fabric marker on assorted green fabrics to make 38 leaves.

4. Scatter leaves in a pleasing arrangement. Pin or baste in place. Refer to Needleturn Appliqué, opposite.

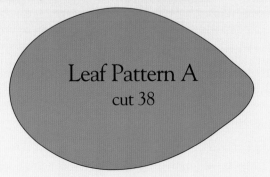

Leaf Pattern A
cut 38

NEEDLETURN APPLIQUÉ

1. Thread a needle with thread to match the appliqué piece. Holding the fabric between thumb and forefinger and using your needle as a tool, fold under a small piece of the seam allowance.

2. Bring the needle up from the background, catching a few threads of the appliqué piece at the fold. Go back into the background where the needle was brought out. Try to keep stitches ⅛" or smaller. Repeat around the appliqué piece.

TIPS
FOR BETTER BORDERS

A vine randomly flowing around a pieced quilt center softens the edges and style of the quilt.

•

Scatter leaves randomly for an eye-pleasing effect.

•

Try a variety of leaves to add visual interest.

•

Choose shapes of oak, maple, ivy, and other leaves from nature.

•

When time is short, machine appliqué leaves and vines.

•

Scraps as small as 2½"x 3½" have big impact as appliquéd leaves.

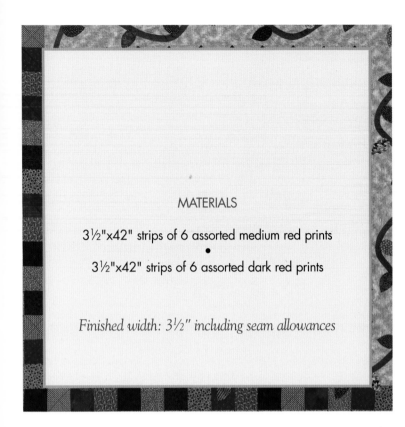

MATERIALS

3½"x42" strips of 6 assorted medium red prints
•
3½"x42" strips of 6 assorted dark red prints

Finished width: 3½" including seam allowances

BORDER FOUR
Squares in a Row

Cutting

From the medium red print strips,
• Cut a total of 34—3½" squares

From the dark red print strips,
• Cut a total of 34—3½" squares

Assembling

Use a ¼" seam allowance for all seams.

1. Randomly alternating the medium red and dark red squares, sew 16 squares into a strip. Repeat to make 2.

2. Sew to the top and bottom of the quilt top.

Continuing to alternate medium and dark squares, sew 18 squares into a strip. Repeat to make 2.

Sew to the sides of the quilt.

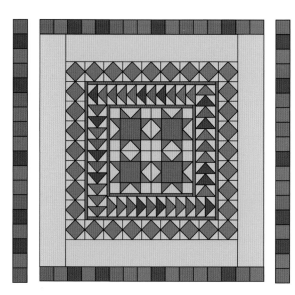

TIPS
FOR BETTER BORDERS

Repeat colors and values from the quilt center to make the quilt style complete.

Arrange squares in a repeating order for a formal look; position them in random order for a more casual folk-art appearance.

Adjust the size of your squares to fit the quilt center.

Make a bold statement with large squares; use small squares for a busy look.

Insert a checkerboard border as a transition between a light center and a dark border. A double row of squares makes a bold border.

MATERIALS

3½"x42" strips of 8 assorted dark purple prints
for diamonds

•

1⅛ yards tan for background

•

2⅜"x42" strip dark green solid for star points

•

4—3½ squares floral border print

Finished width: 6½" including seam allowances

BORDER FIVE
Diamonds with Direction

From tan background,
• Cut 8—3⅞"x42" strips. Cut into 72—3⅞" squares, cut in half diagonally once for 144 half-square triangles.

Diamond Strips

Cutting

From each dark purple print strip,
• Cut 9 of Diamond pattern shown below. (Or, see Jill's Preferred Method, page 59.)

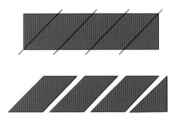

Assembling

Use a ¼" seam allowance for all seams.

1. Sew a tan background triangle to each end of a dark purple diamond. Make 72. Press seams towards diamonds. Units should measure 3½"x6½" including seam allowances. (See Sewing Diamond Units, page 52.)

2. Sew 18 diamond units into a strip as shown. Repeat to make 4 strips.

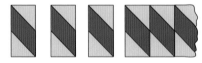

DIAMOND TEMPLATE

BORDER SAMPLER
cut 9 from each of 8 assorted purple prints

SEWING DIAMOND UNITS

1. Align the tan triangle with the angle edge of the purple diamond, offsetting the top corner ¼".

3. Press seams towards the tan triangles. By pressing them in this manner the diamond units seams will join easier. Clip off threads and dogears.

2. Using a ¼" seam allowance, sew the tan triangles to each angled edge of the purple diamond.

4. Finished diamond unit.

Star Corners

Cutting

From the tan background,
- Cut 16—2" squares.
- Cut 4—4¼" squares. Cut in half diagonally twice for 16 quarter-square triangles.

From green solid,
- Cut 16—2⅜" squares. Cut in half diagonally once for 32 half-square triangles.

Assembling

1. Sew 2 green half-square triangles to each tan background triangle, as shown, to make a Flying Geese unit. Make 16. Press seams towards small triangles.

2. For each block arrange 4 Flying Geese, 4 tan squares, and a floral square in rows as shown. Sew the pieces into rows.

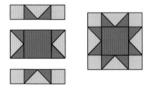

Sew the rows together. Make 4. Block should measure 6½" including seam allowance.

Completing Diamond Border:

1. Sew a Diamond Border strip to the top and bottom of the quilt.

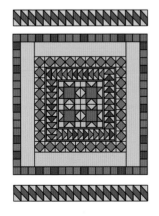

2. Sew a Star Corner to each end of each remaining Diamond Border strip.

3. Sew a strip to each side of the quilt top.

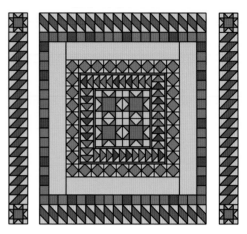

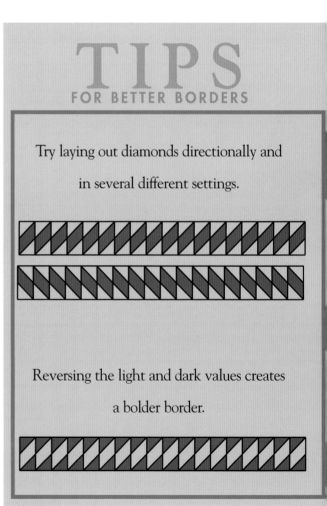

TIPS
FOR BETTER BORDERS

Try laying out diamonds directionally and in several different settings.

Reversing the light and dark values creates a bolder border.

52

MATERIALS

Remaining floral print

Finished width: 6½" including seam allowances

BORDER SIX
Basic Wrap Border

Cutting
From floral print,
• Cut 7—6½"x42" strips

Assembling

Use a ¼" seam allowance for all seams.

1. Cut one 6½"x42" strip into 2—6½"x21" strips. Sew each short strip to a long one and trim to make a 6½"x60½" rectangle. Make 2. Sew rectangles to the top and bottom of the quilt top. Press seams towards the outside border.

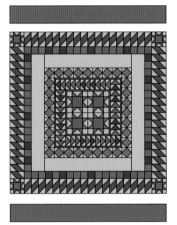

2. Sew 2 strips together and trim to make a 6½"x72½" rectangle. Make 2. Sew the rectangles to the sides of the quilt top. Press the seams towards the outside border.

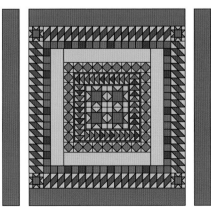

Finishing the Border Sampler:

1. If desired, appliqué vines and leaves as described in Border Three (page 44).

2. Layer, baste, and quilt as desired.

3. Refer to Cross-Grain Double-Fold binding instructions (page 108) to bind quilt with dark green print.

TIPS
FOR BETTER BORDERS

Choose a Basic Wrap Border for easy application or to square up a quilt top and frame a quilt evenly.

•

A Basic Wrap Border uses less fabric than a Mitered Border.

•

Basic Wrap Borders work best with solid fabrics or all-over prints. The busier the print, the less visible the seams appear.

•

Whenever possible use some fabric from the center in the border, or vice-versa—it ties the two together.

Now that you've completed the Working My Way Around *sampler featuring six borders surrounding a center of star blocks, you're ready to use the skills you've learned to make numerous projects shown on the following pages which incorporate the various border techniques from this chapter. After that you'll be ready to add backings, bindings and edgings to your handmade works of art.*

A cheerful table runner inspired by a yellow-and-white print featuring pineapples offers three beautiful borders—pineapple, sawtooth, and rectangles with corner squares.

PINEAPPLE PLEASURES
Table Runner   By Jill Reber

MATERIALS

1¾ yards yellow paisley for diamonds, backing, and binding

•

1¼ yards yellow print for triangles and border

•

¾ yard green plaid for triangles and corner squares

•

Batting to fit finished top

Approximate finished size: 20"x36"

Cutting

From yellow paisley,
• Cut 12 diamonds using Diamond template
• Cut 12 diamonds using Diamond template reversed (See Jill's Preferred Method, Cutting Diamonds, page 59.)

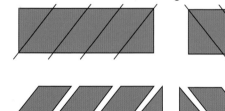

From yellow print,
• Cut 42—2⅞" squares. Cut in half diagonally once for 84 half-square triangles.

• Cut 2—4½"x12½" rectangles
• Cut 2—4½"x28½" rectangles

From green plaid,
• Cut 18—2⅞" squares. Cut in half once diagonally for 36 half-square triangles.

• Cut 4—4½" squares.

Assembling the Pineapple Center
Sew all seams using ¼" seam allowances.

1. Sew a yellow print half-square triangle to each long edge of each Diamond and Diamond reversed, as shown, to make 12 Diamond units and 12 Reversed Diamond units.

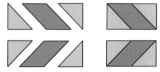

2. Sew a Diamond unit to a Reversed Diamond unit, as shown, to make an inverted V-shaped unit. Make 12.

3. Sew six Inverted V-shaped units together as shown. Repeat to make 2.

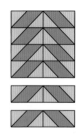

4. Sew the 2 units together as shown.

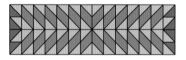

Assembling the Sawtooth Triangle Border
Sew all seams using ¼" seam allowances.

1. Sew each remaining yellow print half-square triangle to a green plaid half-square triangle as shown to make a triangle-square unit.

2. Sew 4 triangle-square units together as shown. Repeat to make 2 border strips.

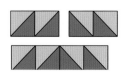

3. Sew one border strip to each short end of the center.

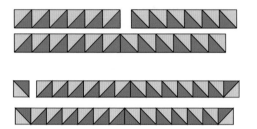

4. Sew 16 triangle-square units together as shown. Repeat to make 2 border strips.

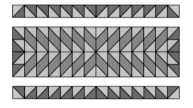

5. Sew one border strip to each long end of the center.

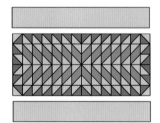

Assembling the Outside Border

Sew all seams using ¼" seam allowances.

1. Sew a 4½"x28½" yellow print rectangle to each long side of the runner. Press seams towards the outside border.

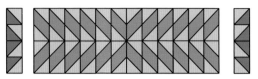

2. Sew a green plaid square to each end of the 4½"x12½" rectangles as shown. Make 2.

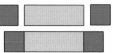

3. Sew to short ends of the runner. Press seams towards the outside border.

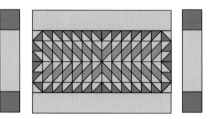

4. Layer, baste and quilt as desired. Bind with Fold-Back-to-Front Binding (page 114) or the binding method of your choice.

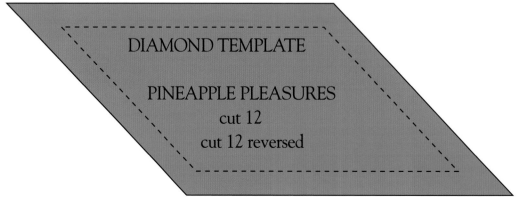

DIAMOND TEMPLATE

PINEAPPLE PLEASURES
cut 12
cut 12 reversed

CUTTING DIAMONDS
JILL'S PREFERRED METHOD

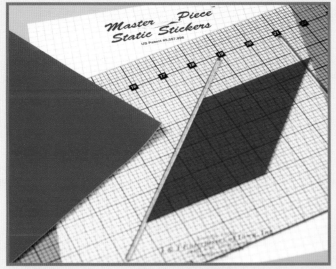

1. For cutting multiples of a template such as the Diamond, opposite, try using template material that sticks to the surface of the ruler such as Master Piece® Static Stickers (mpquilt@aol.com). Transfer pattern templates or draft your own using the graph paper backing. After the template is cut out, the static side clings to the ruler.

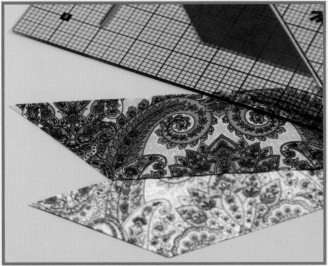

2. Make a template of the Pineapple Diamond from Master Piece® Static Stickers. Cut 2—2½" wide strips. Layer fabric with wrong sides together.

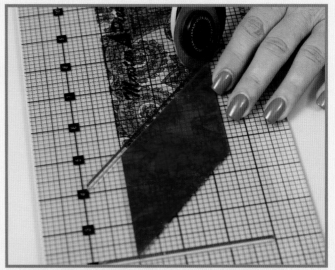

3. Align strips parallel within the lines of the Master Piece 45 JR. Align Static Sticker with angled end of the strip. Cut, running cutter next to the Static Sticker at the edge of the slot.

4. Continue cutting for 12 each diamond and diamond reversed pieces.

Learn two useful border techniques from this eye-catching project! Master mitered corners to enhance striped borders, even when the stripes are subtle. Then practice your appliqué skills on a gracefully curving vine and colorful flowers.

VINE & FLOWERS
Runner
By Margaret Sindelar

MATERIALS

18½" square cream print fabric for center

•

1 yard woven stripe for border

•

½ yard dark green print for vine

•

¼ yard blue print for appliqué flowers

•

⅛ yard pink print for flower centers

•

½ yard pink plaid for bias binding

•

1 yard backing fabric

•

Batting to fit finished quilt top

Approximate finished size: 30"x30"

Cutting

From woven strips,
  Cut 4—6½"x36" strips with the stripes running lengthwise.

Assembling

Use ¼" seam allowance for all seams.

Referring to Building a Mitered Corner, page 62, sew 6½"x36" strips to the square of cream print and miter the corners.

Vine

Cutting

From the green print,
• Cut a 45-degree angle on one edge as shown.

Cut 12—1" bias strips

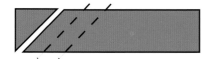

Assembling

1. Sew the strips together to make a bias strip 6½ yards long.

2. Fold the strip in half lengthwise wrong sides together. Machine stitch a scant ⅛" from raw edge. (See Preparing a Vine Appliqué, page 66.)

3. Roll and press stitched line to the back of the bias strip.

4. Trace the vine patterns onto the background border. Arrange the bias strip using the traced lines as a guide. Pin or baste in place.

5. Slip stitch vine in place.

Flowers

Cutting

From blue print,
• Cut 20 of Flower template

From pink print,
• Cut 24 of Center Template

Assembling

Referring to the photos, arrange one Flower, with Center, opposite each small loop of the vine and one Center at each inside corner. Refer to Glossary of Terms (page 132) to hand or machine appliqué flowers.

Finishing

1. Layer, baste and quilt as desired.

2. Cut the pink plaid fabric on the bias. Refer to Cross-Grain Double-Fold Binding (page 108) to make and attach.

BUILDING A MITERED CORNER

1. Mark the ¼"seam allowance with a dot at each corner of quilt center.

3. Keeping first border free, move to the next side of the quilt center. Repeat step 2. Starting and stopping with backstitches, sew between each pair of dots. Clip threads.

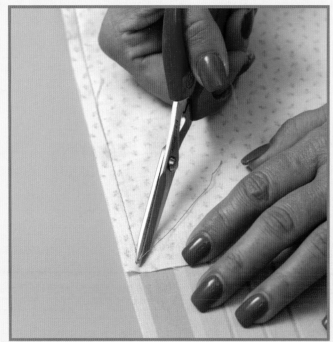

2. Align border strip with edge of quilt, extending the width of the border plus 2" at each end. Pin at dot and then the length of side. Backstitch and sew, starting and stopping at each dot, backstitch. Clip threads. Press towards quilt center.

4. Align two borders one on top of the other, one out straight, one with a 45-degree fold. Press the fold.

5. Fold the creased border over the uncreased one, right sides together, aligning outer border edges.

7. Pin at the crease, making sure to match stripes or patterns of the fabric.

6. Trace the crease with an erasable marker. This will be your sewing line.

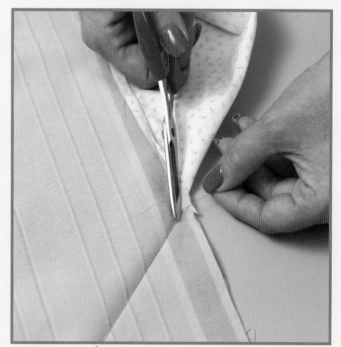

8. Starting ¼" from inner edge, backstitch and sew on drawn line. Trim threads.

BUILDING A MITERED CORNER

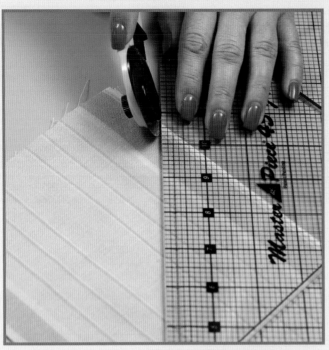

9. Align a rotary ruler and trim ¼" from stitching line. Press the mitered seam open and the border seams toward the border.

11. Trim off excess seam at the outer corner.

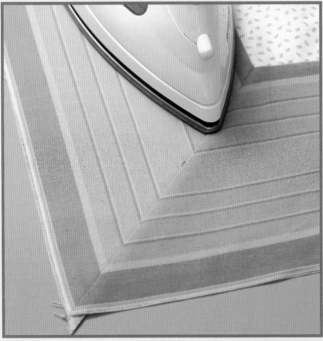

10. From the front, make a final press on the corner.

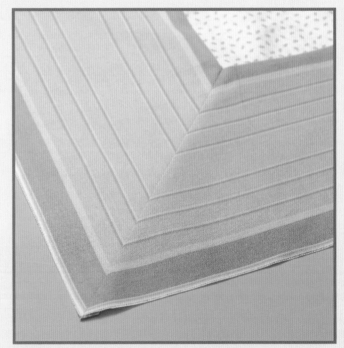

12. Repeat for each corner of the quilt top.

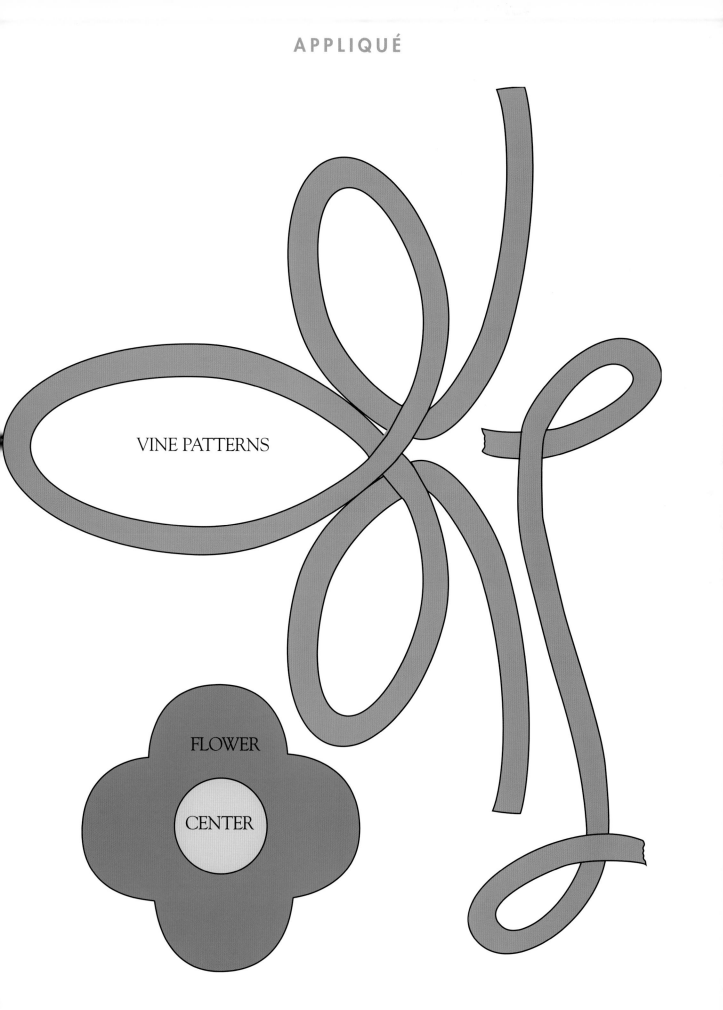

VINE PATTERNS

FLOWER

CENTER

PREPARING A VINE APPLIQUÉ

1. Fold bias strip in half with wrong sides together. Machine stitch a scant ⅛" from raw edge.

3. Using the pattern line provided, trace each corner design onto the border of the quilt top. Trace the inside curves, adjusting as needed. Pin or baste in place.

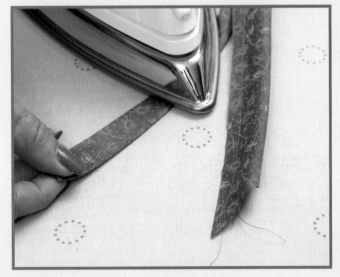

2. Roll the stitched line to the back of the bias strip and press.

4. Slip stitch vine in place.

By Margaret Sindelar

VENETIAN STEPS
Table Runner

Boldly striped fabrics beg to be mitered. Margaret Sindelar went a step further. She fussy-cut wide and narrow strips from a fabric with varying-width stripes and alternated them with two complementary colored fabrics in subtle patterns. Note how Margaret positioned the wide strips so the diamonds form a unique new shape in each corner.

GARDEN'S GLORY
Wall Hanging

Mitered corners add zing to striped fabric borders. Can't find a stripe that suits you? Make your own. Select two muted fabrics to complement a cheery floral. After determining the width of the borders make four identical strips and treat each one as a single fabric strip when you miter the corners.

By Margaret Sindelar

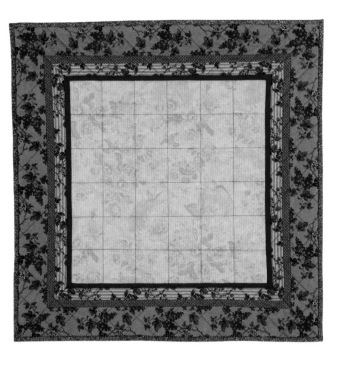

Double-frame a bold scenic print with a simple border surrounded by graceful scallops while you learn the technique of clean-finish edges.

STRAWBERRIES & CREAM
Table Mat
By Margaret Sindelar

MATERIALS

14½" square of red toile print fabric for center

•

¼ yard of dark green print for first border

•

¼ yard red print for pieced border

•

¼ yard light green print for pieced border

•

⅞ yard backing fabric

•

Batting to fit finished quilt top

Approximate finished size: 26"x26"

Cutting

For mitered corners on inside border, from dark green print,
  Cut 4—2½"x22" strips.
Option: For Basic Wrap Border on inside border, from dark
  green print,
  Cut 2—2½"x14½" rectangles
  Cut 2—2½"x18½" rectangles

From red print,
  Cut 12 of Scallop template
  Cut 4 of Corner template

From light green print,
  Cut 16 of Tumbler template

Assembling Inside Border

Use ¼" seam allowances for all seams.

1. For mitered corners as shown in the photograph, see
   Building a Mitered Corner (page 62).

2. For optional Basic Wrap Border, sew the 2—2½"x14½"
   rectangles to the top and bottom of toile center square.
   Press seams towards border. Sew the 2—2½"x18½"
   rectangles to the sides of
   the toile center square.
   Press seams towards
   border.

Assembling Outside Border

Use ¼" seam allowances for all seams.

1. Sew 3 Scallop pieces and 4 Tumbler pieces into one
   Outside Border. Make 4. (See Sewing Irregular Pieces,
   page 72.)

2. Mark the ¼" seam allowance at each corner of the quilt
   center and at each end of the straight edge of Outside
   Border.

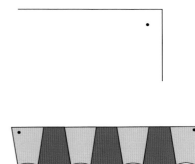

3. Sew the Outside Borders to the sides of the quilt center, starting and stopping at the ¼" marked seam allowance. Press seam towards the First Border.

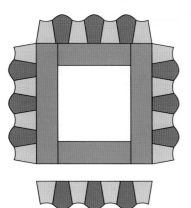

4. To inset corners smoothly, mark the ¼" seam allowance at the points of the Corner pieces. With the Corner piece on top, sew one straight edge, starting at the ¼" mark. Sew second straight edge. Repeat on all 4 corners.

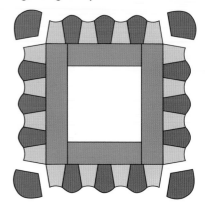

Finishing

1. Layer, baste, and quilt as desired.

2. Refer to Irregular Clean Finish (page 127) to clean finish the outside of the quilt.

SEWING IRREGULAR PIECES

1. Combining these three pattern pieces creates a smooth undulating curve on this graceful border.

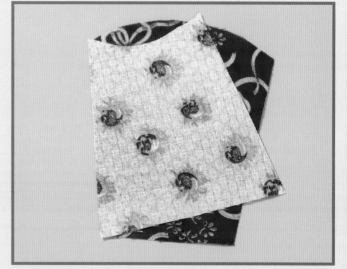

2. Align the straight edges with the Tumbler piece on top. The curved ends of the two pieces should only meet ¼" from the straight edge.

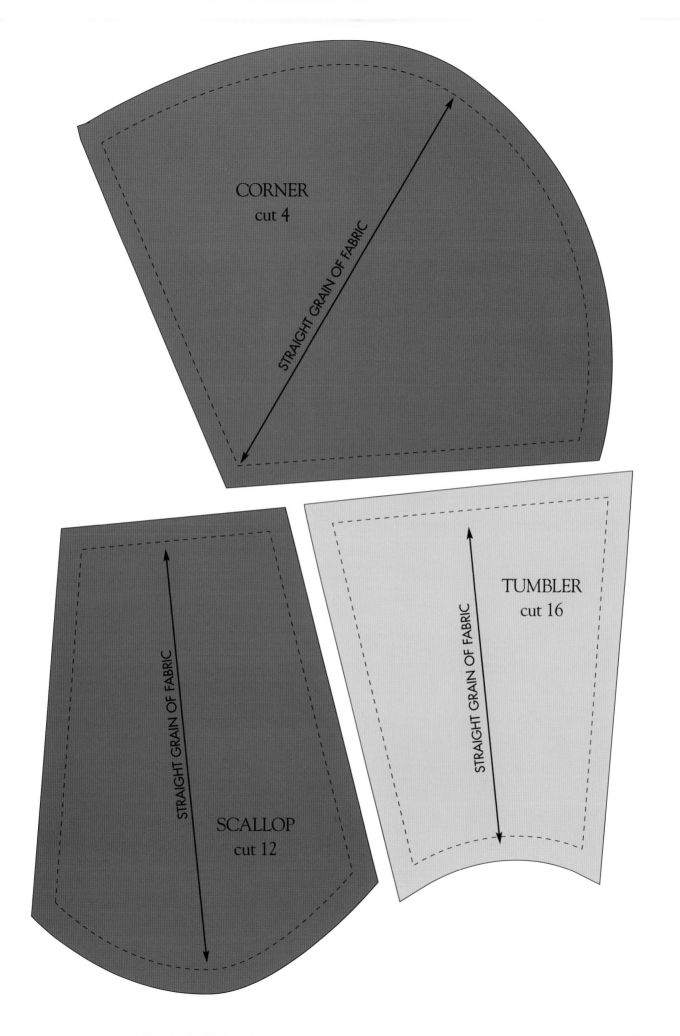

CORNER
cut 4

STRAIGHT GRAIN OF FABRIC

SCALLOP
cut 12

STRAIGHT GRAIN OF FABRIC

TUMBLER
cut 16

STRAIGHT GRAIN OF FABRIC

For a little night music add a piano-key border to a winter warmer featuring a weathervane star. This scrappy quilt with corner blocks on the border is a stash-keeper's delight.

WEATHERVANE STAR
Lap Quilt
By Jill Reber

MATERIALS

¼ yard each of 9 different medium/dark prints
for star points

•

¼ yard each of 9 different medium/dark prints
for block centers

•

⅓ yard each of 9 different tan prints
for background

•

3 yards backing

•

Batting to fit finished top

Approximate finished size: 52"x52"

Cutting

For best use of fabric, cut all pieces in order given.

From each of the 9 different medium/dark star-point prints,
  Cut 1—2½"x42" strip; set aside for binding. Trim remaining
  piece to 6½"x42".
  Cut 4—2½"x6½" rectangles for the Piano-Key border. Trim
  to 5¼".
  Cut 2—5¼" squares. Cut in half diagonally twice for 8
  quarter-square triangles. Trim piece to 2⅞".
• Cut 4—2⅞" squares, cut in half diagonally once for 8
  half-square triangles.

From scraps of star-point prints,
  Cut 4—2⅞" squares. Cut in half once diagonally for 8
  half-square triangles; set aside.

From each of the 9 different medium/dark block-center prints,
• Cut 1—2½"x42" strip. Cut 4—2½" squares. Set aside the
  rest of the strips for binding. Trim remaining piece to
  6½"x42".
• Cut 5—2½"x6½" rectangles for the Piano-Key border. Trim
  remaining piece to 4½".
  Cut 1—4½" square.

From scraps of the block-center prints,
• Cut 4—2½" squares; set aside.

From each of the 9 different tan prints,
• Cut 1—2½"x42" strip. Cut 4—2½" squares. Set aside the
  rest of the strip for first border. Trim remaining piece to
  5¼"x42."
• Cut 2—5¼" squares. Cut in half diagonally twice for 8
  quarter-square triangles. Trim piece to 2⅞".
• Cut 4—2⅞" squares. Cut in half diagonally once for 8
  half-square triangles.

From scraps of the tan prints,
• Cut 4—2½" squares
• Cut 4—2⅞" squares. Cut in half once diagonally for 8
  half-square triangles; set aside.

Blocks

Assembling

Use a ¼" seam allowance for all seams.

1. Omitting pieces for binding, Piano-Key border, and first
   border, group fabrics into 9 block sets.

2. For each block, sew a tan half-square triangle to a star-
   point half-square triangle, as shown, to make a triangle
   square. Repeat to make 8.

3. Sew 2 triangle squares, 1—2½" tan square and 1—2½"
   star-center square together as shown, to make an A unit.
   Make 4.

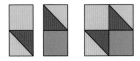

4. Sew 2 star-point quarter-square triangles to 2 tan quarter-square triangles, as shown, to make a B unit. Make 4.

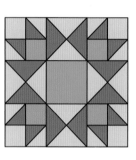

5. Arrange the A units, the B units, and a 4½" block-center square as shown. Sew the units together in rows. Sew the rows together. Block should measure 12½" including seam allowances.

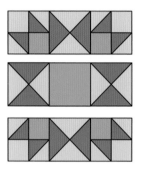

6. Arrange the blocks as shown. Sew together in rows.

First Border

Assembling

1. Cut the reserved 2½" tan strips into random lengths.

2. Sew the strips together to make 2—36½" lengths. Sew to top and bottom of the quilt top.

3. Sew the remaining tan strips together to make 2—40½" lengths. Sew to sides of quilt top.

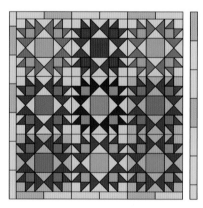

Piano-Key Border

Assembling

ew 20 of the reserved 2½"x6½" rectangles together in
ndom order as shown. Make 4. Sew a Piano-Key border to
e top and bottom of the quilt top; set the remaining Piano-
ey borders aside.

Corner Units

Assembling

. Sew the pieces cut from scraps (star-point half-square
  triangles, tan half-square triangles, tan squares, and block
  center squares) together to make 4 A units.

. From the strips reserved for binding, randomly choose and
  cut 4—2½"x4½" rectangles. Sew one rectangle to the side
  of each A unit as shown. Cut 4—2½"x6½" rectangles, sew
  the top of each unit as shown.

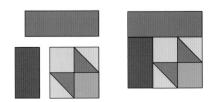

3. Sew a Corner unit to each end of one Piano-Key border
   unit as shown. Repeat to make 2.

4. Sew the Corner Units/Piano-Key borders to the sides of the
   quilt top as shown.

5. Layer, baste, and quilt as desired. Sew random lengths of
   the set-aside 2½" strips and use to make and apply Cross-
   Grain Double-Fold binding (page 108) or the binding
   method of your choice.

Bring blooms and blossoms to your table on a table runner that features simple appliqué and patchwork, plus easy-to-make curved corner blocks.

ORANGE BLOSSOM
Table Runner   By Margaret Sindelar

MATERIALS

9½"x20" rectangle medium yellow print for blocks

•

6½"x18" rectangle light yellow print for blocks

•

3"x21" rectangle orange print for Four-Patch Units

•

3"x21" rectangle tan paisley print for Four Patch Units

•

Scraps of orange, green and red prints for appliqué

•

1½ yards green stripe for borders, piping, and backing

•

3¼ yards ⅛"-diameter cording for piping

•

Batting to fit finished quilt top

Approximate finished size: 18"x34"

Cutting

From medium yellow print,
  Cut 2—8⅞" squares. Cut in half diagonally once for 4 half-square triangles. (You will only use 3 half-square triangles.)

From light yellow print,
  Cut 3—4⅞" squares. Cut in half diagonally once for 6 half-square triangles.

From orange print,
• Cut 6—2½" squares

From tan paisley,
• Cut 6—2½" squares

From green border stripe,
• Cut 2—5½"x8½" rectangles
• Cut 2—5½"x24½" rectangles
• Cut 4—5½" squares on the bias
• Cut 18"x42" strip for piping

Assembling

Use ¼" seam allowance for all seams.

1. Referring to Glossary of Terms (page 132) for machine or hand appliqué, center a flower on the long edge of each medium yellow triangle. For machine appliqué, add a ¼" seam allowance to the bottom edge of the flower stem. For hand appliqué, do not turn the bottom of the stem seam allowance under. Align the cut edges of the stem seam allowance and the medium yellow triangle. Sew, using your chosen method. Make 3.

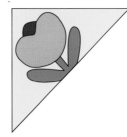

2. Sew 2 orange print squares and 2 tan paisley squares together to make a Four Patch unit. Make 3.

3. Sew a light yellow triangle to two sides of each Four Patch unit as shown. Press seams towards the triangles.

4. Sew the pieced unit to the appliqué unit as shown. Block should measure 8½" including seam allowances.

5. Sew the three blocks together, alternating direction, as shown.

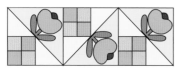

6. Sew a 5½"x8½" green stripe rectangle to each short side of the table runner.

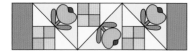

7. Sew a 5½" green stripe square to the short end of a 5½"x24½" rectangle. Repeat to make 2.

8. Sew to the long side of the table runner. Press seams towards border. Trim the corner squares to a quarter circle. (See Margaret's Preferred Method—Rounded Corners, right.)

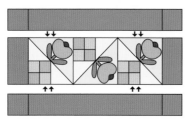

9. For piping, cut a 45-degree angle on one edge of the 18"x42" strip of green stripe. Aligning ruler with the diagonal edge, cut 5—1"-wide strips.

10. Referring to the instructions for Bias Piping (page 125) us the 1"-wide strips and the ⅛"-diameter cording to prepar 3¼ yards of piping.

11. Use the table runner as a pattern to cut batting and backing; set backing aside. Align the table runner, right side up, on the batting. Sew the piping to the right side of the table runner at the outside edges. Trim batting close to the stitching.

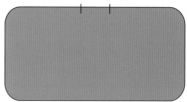

12. With right sides together, sew the back to the front, stitching on the piping line and leaving an opening on on long side for turning.

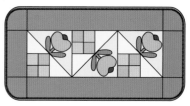

13. Trim and clip seam allowance at the rounded corners.

14. Turn table runner right side out through the opening. Press table runner. Slip stitch opening closed(see Glossary of Terms, page 135).

15. Quilt as desired.

ROUNDED CORNERS
MARGARET'S PREFERRED METHOD

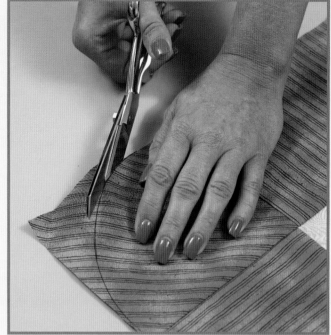

1. For a template, choose a household item (plate, bowl, or lid) about 11" in diameter. Position it on the corner so the edges of the plate touch the outer edges at the seam lines of the square. Trace the edge of the template with a fabric marker.

2. Following drawn line, trim away the excess fabric.

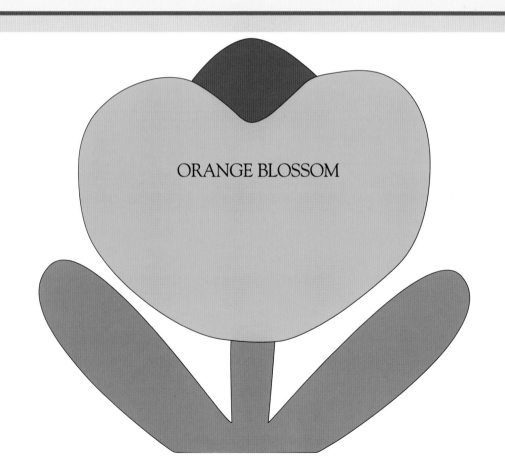

ORANGE BLOSSOM

It's easy to visualize these interlocking circles, adapted from an antique quilt, extending all the way around a simple quilt. To help you master the graceful curved edges, we've included full-size patterns and some special helps. Want to add interest to a quilt center with straight edges? Simply square off the edge of the melon pieces that connect to the quilt.

GLORIFIED NINE PATCH
Runner
By Margaret Sindelar

MATERIALS

6½"x20" rectangle of red print for block

•

6½"x20" rectangle of purple print for block

•

6½"x20" rectangle of pink print for block

•

3"x42" strip of tan print for blocks

•

½ yard floral print for melon border

•

½ yard rust print for bias binding

•

½ yard backing fabric

•

Batting to fit finished quilt top

Approximate finished size: 13"x32"

Cutting

From red, purple, and pink print,
• Cut 4 pieces each using Kite template.
• Cut 1—2½" square each.

From tan print,
• Cut 12—2½" squares.

From floral print,
• Cut 10 pieces using Melon template.

Assembling

Use a ¼" seam allowance for all seams.

1. Sew the red, purple, or pink kite pieces, 2½" squares, and the tan 2½" squares together in rows as shown. Sew the rows together to make a Nine Patch unit.

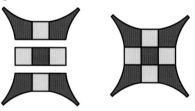

2. Sew a Melon piece to each curved edge of the red Glorified Nine Patch unit as shown (see Sewing Curved Pieces, page 85).

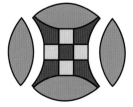

3. Sew a Melon piece to 3 sides of the purple and pink Nine-Patch units.

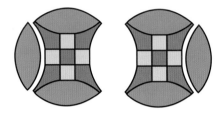

4. Sew the purple Glorified Nine-Patch unit to the left Melon unit of the red Glorified Nine-Patch unit as shown. Sew the pink Glorified Nine-Patch unit to the right Melon unit side of the Glorified Nine-Patch unit.

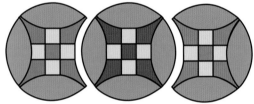

Finishing

1. Layer, baste, and quilt as desired.

2. Refer to Double-Fold Bias Binding (page 112) to make and attach rust print binding.

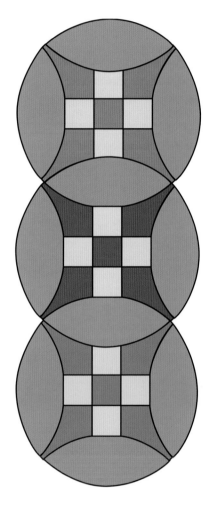

SEWING CURVED PIECES

1. Here's how to sew a concave curve like the edges of this Nine Patch unit to a convex curve like the Melon pieces.

2. Mark the center of the Nine Patch unit with a fabric marker.

3. Fold the Melon piece in half bringing the points together and mark by creasing at the fold.

4. With right sides together, and the Nine Patch unit on top, pin the two marks together. Pin pieces at the seam line at each end of the curve.

5. Sew slowly, keeping the raw edges aligned and stopping after every few stitches to adjust the fullness of the Nine Patch unit.

6. Press seams towards the Melon pieces.

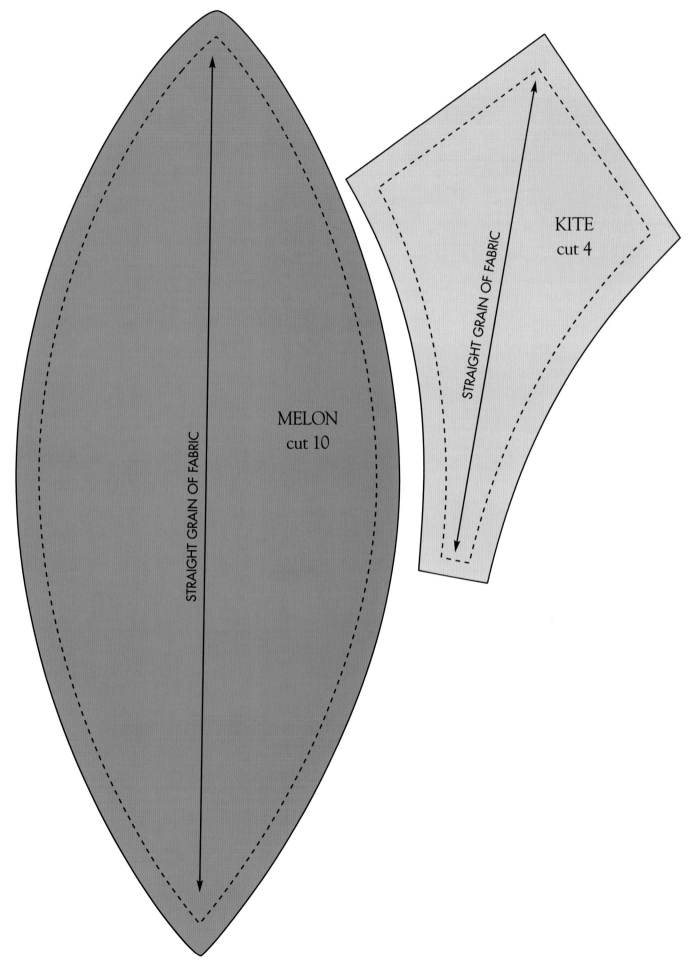

MELON
cut 10

STRAIGHT GRAIN OF FABRIC

KITE
cut 4

STRAIGHT GRAIN OF FABRIC

There's plenty of block and border interest in this patchwork table topper. Best of all, these stripes and checks are so easy to make you'll want to use the technique often.

CHECKERBOARD STAR
Table Topper   By Jill Reber

MATERIALS

1 yard floral print for blocks, backing and binding

•

¼ yard blue print for star points

•

¼ yard red print for border

•

¼ yard tan print for border

•

Batting to fit finished top

Approximate finished size: 24"x24"

Cutting

From floral print,
  Cut 16—2½" squares
  Cut 4—4½" squares
  Cut 4—5¼" squares. Cut in half diagonally twice for 16
  quarter-square triangles.

From blue print,
  Cut 16—2⅞" squares. Cut in half diagonally once for 32
  half-square triangles.

Assembling

Sew all seams using ¼" seam allowances.

1. Sew 2 blue half-square triangles to each floral print
   triangle, as shown, to make a Flying Geese unit. Make 16.

Press seams towards small triangles.

3. For each block arrange 4 Flying Geese, 4 —2½" floral
   print squares, and a 4½" floral print square in rows as
   shown. Sew the pieces into rows. Sew the rows together.
   Make 4.

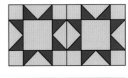

4. Sew the 4 blocks together as shown.

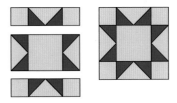

Border and Corners

Cutting

From tan print,
• Cut 5—1½"x42" strips

From red print,
• Cut 5—1½"x42" strips

Assembling

Use a ¼" seam allowance for all seams.

1. Use 2 tan print strips and 2 red strips to make a strip set as shown. Press seams toward the red. Make 2.

2. Cut the remaining strips in half and make a 1½"x21" strip set.

3. From the 42" strip sets cut 4—16½" lengths.

4. From the remaining pieces cut 16—1½" units. Sew 4 units into a Checkerboard unit. Make 4.

5. Sew a 16½" border unit to the top and bottom of the Star Center, as shown. Press seams towards border.

6. Sew a Checkerboard unit to each end at the remaining 16½" border units.

7. Sew to the sides of Star Center. Press seams towards borders.

8. Layer, baste and quilt as desired. Bind with Fold-Back-to-Front Binding (page 114) or the binding method of your choice.

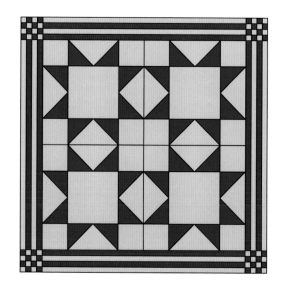

CHECKERBOARD CORNERS

1. From the 42" strip sets cut 4—16½" lengths. Set aside. From the remaining strip sets, cut 16—1½" wide pieces.

3. Rotate the Checkerboard unit so the adjacent colors alternate with the strip set.

2. Arrange the 1½" pieces alternately into 4 x 4-square Checkerboard units. Sew the rows together.

Backings

The beauty of the quilt back is at its best when it blends in color, style, and design with the quilt top. There are many useful ways to make the back an interesting addition to your quilt. To keep it plain and simple, purchase extra-wide fabric for a whole-cloth backing. For more ideas—from backings with large-scale prints, random horizontals, verticals, or diagonals to pillow ticking and enlarged blocks—or for tips for adding a hanging sleeve, take a tour of our gallery.

Front of the quilt

Back of the quilt

backings with
WHOLE CLOTH

If quilting by hand or machine, a whole-cloth back is the ultimate way to show off your workmanship. The quilt can be as simple as two large pieces of fabric or you can make a double-duty quilt with patchwork and/or appliqué on the front.

If you're hand-quilting, consider extra-wide fabric, available where most quilting supplies are sold. Muslin is available in widths from 90-116" and more prints in the extra-wide fabric are becoming available all the time.

backings with
LARGE-SCALE PRINTS

One of the quickest ways to make a bold statement on the back of a quilt is with a large-scale print.

These are often theme-styled fabrics and come in a multitude of designs, colors and styles. The fabrics can be seamed and redesigned to fit and coordinate with your quilt top.

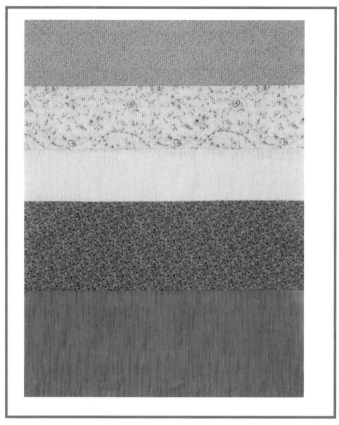

backings with
TWO SEAMS

If your quilt is bed size and the fabric you've chosen is only available in 45" width, two seams are better than one. For quilts that are less than about 85 inches, split one fabric lengthwise to produce a back proportioned like the one shown above. For very large quilts, sew three full widths of fabric together.

The two-fabric back shown above produces a casual look, while using the same fabric throughout lends a more formal styling.

backings with
RANDOM HORIZONTALS OR VERTICALS

Sewing random widths of fabric together—either horizontally or vertically to fit your quilt top— can be a thrifty way to use up left-over pieces from other projects.

Make sure seams lay flat and will not fall too close to the edge of the quilt top. Be sure to press seams out from the center.

95

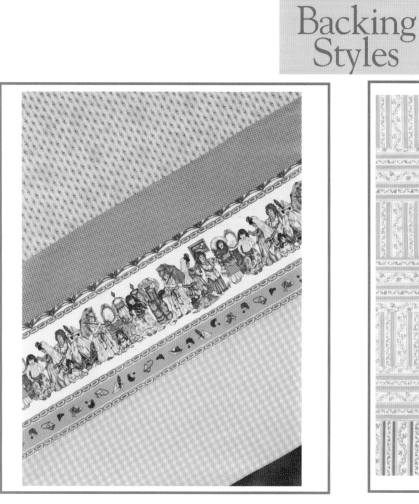

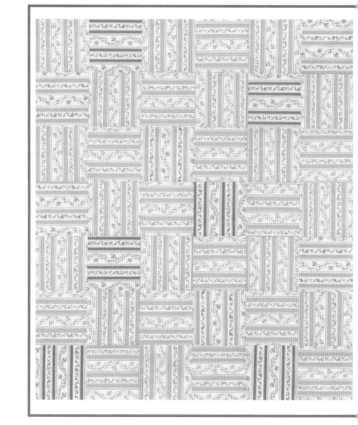

backings with
RANDOM DIAGONALS

Sewing random widths of fabric together on the diagonal to fit your quilt top is another thrifty and interesting way to use up random fabrics leftover from other projects. Keep in mind that backs with lots of seams are better candidates for machine quilting than hand. Trim the back square before basting with quilt top.

backings with
PILLOW TICKING

For this example, 6½" squares of three different pillow-ticking style prints were cut and randomly seamed back together. Don't stop with ticking. Any size squares cut of a striped fabric look sensational!

backings with
ENLARGED BLOCKS

A quilt top can be inspiration for a quilt back when a simple block design is used. Enlarge the block as needed to a sufficient size. Add several borders to increase to the size of the back. The final border should be large enough to allow for centering the quilt top with excess to be trimmed off.

backings with
RANDOM SCRAPS

Using random scraps from a quilt top makes an interesting back. Adding angled ends to fabrics in various shades increases visual interest. Sew these angled strips together into rows several inches wider than your quilt top. Then sew the rows together, squaring up the sides when completed.

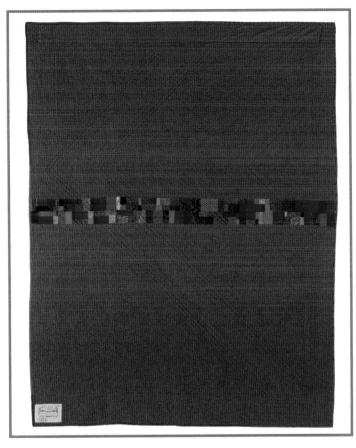

a back with
INSPIRATION

This quilt back uses extra strip sets from the quilt front to create extra length and coordinate the back with the front. Imagine a row of patchwork blocks or a strip of appliquéd flowers instead. Let necessity be your guide to the strip width and consider a vertical row when needed.

Notice that this quilt was designed as a wall quilt with a matching hanging sleeve at the top.

Adding a Hanging Sleeve

A sleeve for displaying a quilt on a rod can be added to any quilt, any time, even an antique or a new quilt that has been bound. For fun, we added decorative machine stitches to the one shown below. To add a sleeve before binding, see Tools and Terms, page 133.

1. Cut a strip 8½" wide and 1" shorter than the finished width of the quilt.

2. Hem the short edges by pressing the raw edge under ½" twice. Topstitch in place using decorative stitches, if desired. With right sides together, fold the strip in half lengthwise and sew the long edges together using a ¼" seam and backstitching at each end. Turn the tube right side out. Press in half so the seam is centered between pressed edges. Embellish with decorative threads and stitches, if desired. Center one long pressed edge adjacent to the binding at the top of the quilt and pin.

3. Slip stitch each long edge of the tube to the quilt.

Basic Rules and Sizes of Backs

To allow for stretching or shifting while quilting and to allow for putting the quilt on a large quilt frame, a quilt back needs to be 4" to 6" larger all around than the quilt top.

STANDARD SIZES					
	CRIB	TWIN	FULL	QUEEN	KING
Mattress dimensions	27" x 52"	39" x 75"	54" x 75"	60" x 80"	76" x 80"
Approximate size of finished quilt top to be used with dust ruffle	39" x 58"	60" x 96"	80" x 96"	90" x 100"	104" x 104"
Approximate finished backing size	45" x 64"	66" x 102"	86" x 102"	96" x 106"	110" x 110"
Approximate total yards of 44-45" wide fabric needed	1¾ yards	4 yards	6 yards	9 yards	9½ yards
Seam as needed to fit quilt top					

1 Keep backs flat and seams pressed flat. Press seams out from center.

2 If your back has many seams it may be difficult to hand quilt, unless the seams are strategically placed. Machine quilting works well for pieced backs.

3 Be sure to keep the back and quilt top well aligned while basting. This can be accomplished by working with clamps on a table or flat on a floor.

4 Wide fabric 90"–116" is available where quilting supplies are sold.

5 If you choose to take your quilt to a professional long-arm machine quilter, ask before you layer and baste the back, batting, and top. Most long-arm machines don't require that step.

Bindings

The final framework for your quilt is the binding which holds all the layers of your quilt together to give it a clean-finished edge. To make a finishing statement with the binding for your quilt, explore several interesting options including Cross-Grain Double Fold Binding, Bias Double Fold Binding and Back-to-Front Binding.

bindings with
CROSS-GRAIN DOUBLE FOLD

Quilts with square corners are easily bound using Cross-Grain Double Fold Binding. This application lends itself to many fabric choices. Consider using random scraps to repeat the colors and values from your finished quilt. Follow the instructions on page 108 to help you complete a perfect binding.

bindings with
BIAS
DOUBLE FOLD

Quilts with gentle curves, rounded edges, and irregular edges usually require a Double Fold Bias Binding. The bias allows for the necessary ease and stretch while applying and turning the binding. Bias plaid and striped fabrics can be applied to the long straight edges of almost any quilt. Follow the step-by-step instructions on page 112 to finish your quilt with bias perfection.

bindings with
BACK-TO-FRONT
FOLD

Knowing this quick-and-easy machine sewing technique will
prove very useful. For the back-to-front fold, choose a
companion or complementary fabric, or buy extra yardage of
fabric used on the quilt top. Extend the backing fabric by just
a few inches beyond the edges of your quilt top. Layer the
backing and top with batting. Quilt, trim up the back, fold,
press, and stitch. It's a quick, clean finish for the busy quilter.

CROSS-GRAIN DOUBLE FOLD

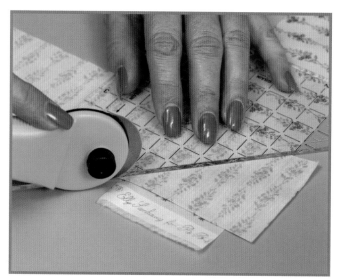

1. Cut the needed number of strips. Lay strips right sides together, at right angles to one another and cut a 45-degree angle across.

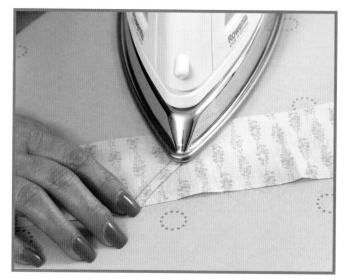

3. Press seams to one side.

2. Sew strips right sides together, offsetting the seam.

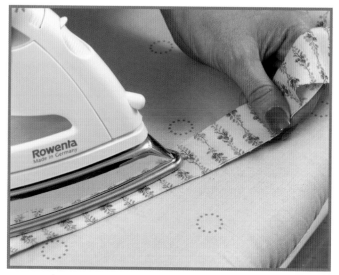

4. Press the sewn strips in half lengthwise, right side out.

5. For a clean edge to start. Fold down one end at a 45-degree angle, press.

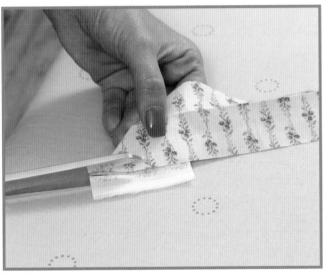

6. Trim off the selvage edge.

7. Refold along the lengthwise crease; press.

8. (No Photo) For binding that was cut 2½", use a ⅜" seam allowance. If your binding is wider or narrower you will need to adjust your seam allowance accordingly. A walking foot is helpful when sewing the binding to the quilt. Working on the right side of your quilt, start at the center of the bottom edge with the folded end.

9. As you approach the corner, place a pin ⅜" from the edge.

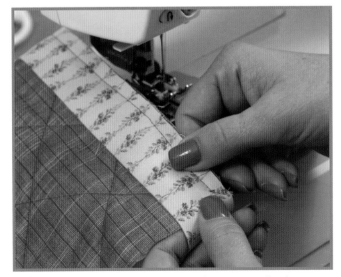

10. Sew to the pin. Stop sewing with your needle down. Pivot and sew off edge to the corner, as shown.

11. Remove quilt from machine, clip threads. Fold binding away from the quilt at a 45-degree angle.

12. Fold back towards the quilt again, aligning fold with outside edge of corner. Pin.

13. Start at edge and sew, continuing down the next side. Repeat for all sides and corners of quilt.

14. To end the binding, stop sewing with needle down. Lay the binding end over the beginning diagonal flap. Trim away the excess end of the binding at the point where the beginning seam and the diagonal flap intersect. Finish sewing the end of the binding.

15. Remove the quilt from the machine. Separate the cut end from the beginning flap.

16. Tuck the cut end of the binding into the flap.

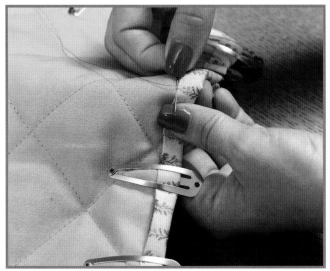

17. Hand-stitch the binding to back side of the quilt using small slip stitches. Binding clips can be used to help keep binding in place as you stitch.

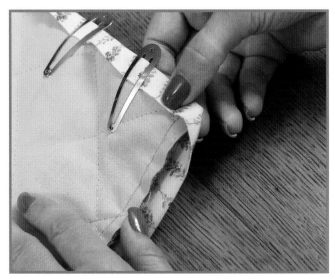

18. For corners, fold down forming an angle on the edge of the unturned binding and finger crease.

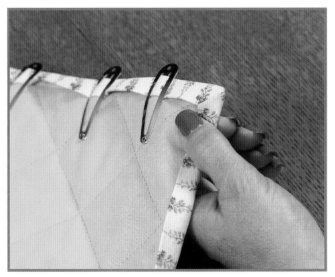

19. Fold the binding toward the quilt back, forming a miter at the corner.

BIAS DOUBLE FOLD

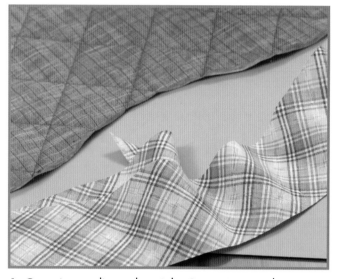

1. Cut strips as directed at right. Sew strips together in a continuous strip as directed for Double Fold Cross-Grain steps 2–7 (pages 108–109) except after pressing one end at 45-degree angle, trim the end even with the length of the strip.

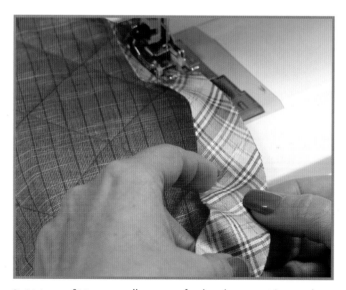

2. Using a ⅜" seam allowance for binding cut 2½" wide, begin sewing as directed for Double Fold Cross-Grain step 9 (page 109). Ease the cut edges of the bias to fit around outside curves.

MATERIALS

To cut 2½"-wide binding strips for a crib or lap quilt, purchase ½ yard of 42"-wide fabric, which will produce 25" strips. For larger quilts, you'll need a one yard piece.

Measure the outside edges of your finished quilt. If you're cutting plaid or stripe fabric for a straight-edge quilt or your quilt has simple rounded corners, use the formula on page 108. For scalloped or irregular edges, it's a good idea to use a tape measure around the curves. Round measurements up for insurance.

To determine the number of strips needed, divide the outside measurement by 25.
Cut the strips to the desired width. If needed, you can also cut shorter strips from the corner pieces of the fabric.

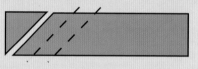

3. Gently stretch the fabric into inside curves. If the inside curve is actually pointed, stop with the needle down and pivot. Finish the binding as directed for Double Fold Cross-Grain steps 14–16 (page 110).

Beautiful Trim Ideas with Double-Fold Binding

Add dimension to your binding by accenting it with
a variety of trims and embellishments.

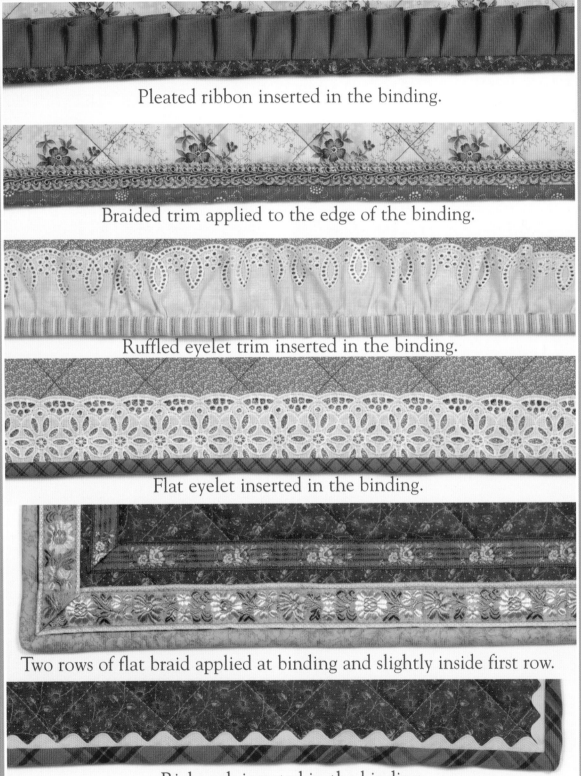

Pleated ribbon inserted in the binding.

Braided trim applied to the edge of the binding.

Ruffled eyelet trim inserted in the binding.

Flat eyelet inserted in the binding.

Two rows of flat braid applied at binding and slightly inside first row.

Rick rack inserted in the binding.

BACK TO FRONT

3. Fold binding to front, raw edges even with edges of quilt top, and press. Repeat for all sides.

Square Corner

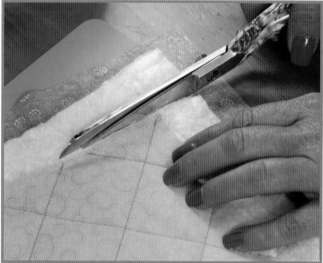

1. Quilt as desired to the edges of the top. Leave batting and backing around the quilt top unstitched. Trim batting even with the quilt top.

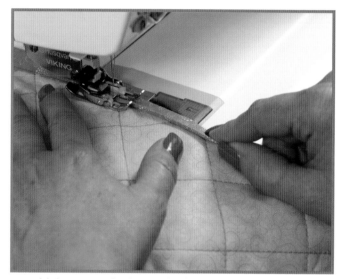

4. Fold the pressed edge to the front, forming a second fold at the edge of the quilt top. Using a walking foot, stitch close to the pressed edge. Straight or decorative stitches may be used. Or, hand stitch just through the quilt top.

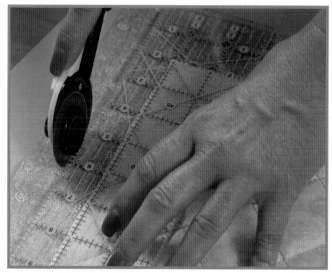

2. Trim off backing fabric evenly, measuring from edge of quilt top, twice the width of desired binding.

5. Make square corners by first turning opposite sides of the quilt and finishing. Then repeat for the other two sides.

Mitered Corner

1. Prepare the backing as shown in Square Corner steps 1 and 2. Press one edge even with the quilt top. Pressing lines will be used to line up the miter.

2. Fold next edge over as shown.

3. Unfold the pressed edges. Bring the backing corner to the quilt front, using pressed lines as a guide, then re-press sides.

4. Trim off excess corner fabric between the two sides.

5. Finish pressing the backing forward at the corner. Pin and repeat for each corner.

6. Hand or machine stitch in place.

Edgings

For a fantastic finish, add easy or elegant edgings to the binding of the quilt. On the following pages you'll find imaginative and versatile ideas ranging from Prairie Points to piping and edgings with irregular clean finishes and yo-yo trims.

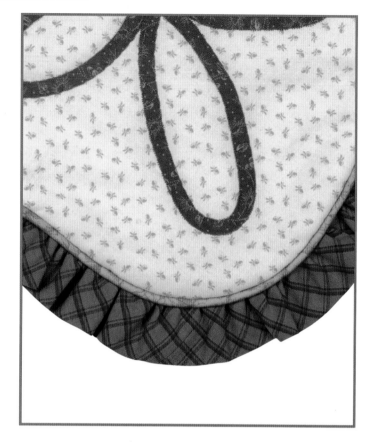

edgings with
PRAIRIE POINTS

Prairie Points add a pleasing geometric edge to a quilt. Made of folded fabric, they were a favorite finish for pioneer quilters. Although they're usually seen zigzagging beyond the outer seam of a quilt as pictured, a row of Prairie Points can also be sewn between borders or inside the binding, adding a three-dimensional texture to a simple border.

edgings with
PIPING

Piping is another three-dimensional finish, but its dainty roundness softens edges, even when the piping is created from a bold outlining color. Choose solid colors, small prints, plaids, and stripes for textured piping. Piping can be inserted into almost any seam.

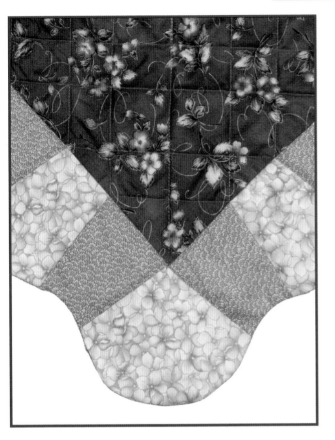

edgings with
IRREGULAR CLEAN FINISH

A few borders can stand alone without binding—those with very small curves or geometric edges are especially spectacular all by themselves. Clean-finish the borders' irregular edges and let them radiate their star power.

edgings with
YO-YO TRIMS

In the 1930s the "waste not, want not" philosophy inspired some interesting quilt patterns including yo-yos cut from small circles of fabric scraps. With more time than money, yo-yo quilts were one of the most enduring. Although today not many quilters take the time to make complete bed covers from these tiny scraps of fabric, the appeal of yo-yo trims as an embellishment remains strong.

Prairie points can be folded several ways. Instructions for classic Quarter-Square Prairie Points, shown above, are on page 122. Another technique, Flying Geese Prairie Points, opposite, is especially interesting when striped or plaid fabric is used.

PRAIRIE POINT EDGES

Flying Geese Prairie Points

1. Cut squares desired size. Fold each one in half to form a rectangle; press.

3. Repeat for other corner. Align all raw edges. Sew together in a chain to apply to the quilt, if desired.

2. Fold down one corner, aligning raw edges; press.

4. Quilt the top to within ¾" to 1" from outside edge. Trim top, batting, and backing even. Pin Prairie Point raw edges even with the raw edges of the quilt top and batting only. Be sure the back is not attached.

5. Sew Prairie Points in place, keeping back free.

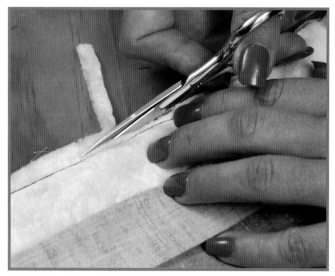

6. Trim batting to stitching line.

7. Working from the backside of the quilt, fold Prairie Points outward. Fold under the backing fabric to the stitched line. Press if desired. Slip stitch all around quilt (see Terms and Tools, page 135).

8. Complete quilting to edge of quilt if desired.

Quarter-Square Prairie Points

1. Cut squares to desired size. Fold in half to form a triangle.

2. Fold again, aligning raw edges. Follow steps 4–8 to attach Prairie Points to quilt.

Piping is a versatile edging for a quilt. Choose a style and color to complement or harmonize with your quilt top, attach piping to a straight or curved edge, and use it with or without binding.

PIPING WITH BINDING

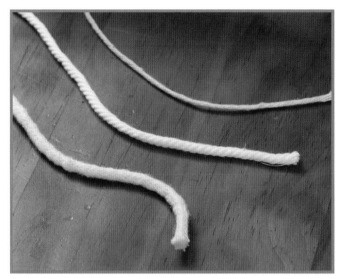

1. Cording filler determines the finished thickness of piping, but will compact slightly when sewn.

2. You may want to experiment with several sizes and choose the size and look that best fits your project.

3. Cut bias strips wide enough to cover the cording and allow for the seam allowance. Cut and sew bias strips together as shown in Terms and Tools (page 132).

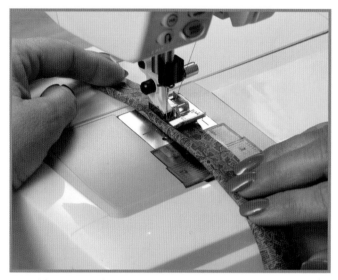

4. Fold wrong sides over cording. Keep raw edges even. Use a cording or zipper foot to sew close to the cording.

5. Stitch piping to the right side of quilt using a zipper foot. Use the stitching line as a guide. At the corner clip to within a few threads of the stitched line and turn corner. Sew desired binding or edging next to the piping.

Quilts that have irregular edges can be very difficult to turn and bind. A clean edge is achieved by using this method shown opposite.

IRREGULAR CLEAN FINISH

3. Trim backing fabric ¼" to ⅜" beyond the edge of the trimmed batting.

1. Turn the raw edge of the quilt top under ¼". Basting this edge is helpful.

4. Roll backing fabric over batting. Backing edges should align with the basted edge of the quilt top. Slip stitch the edges together around the quilt, holding all layers together (see Terms and Tools page 135).

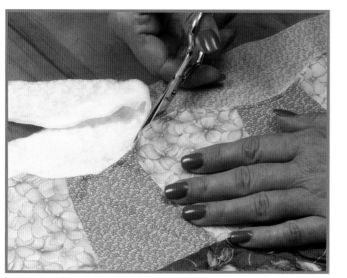

2. Trim batting even with the edge of the basted edge of the quilt top.

5. You now have a clean finished edge. Press if desired.

Yo-Yos are commonly used for making entire coverlets and for embellishments in appliqué. For another option consider adding Yo-Yos to a quilt's finished edge. Use your imagination with the Yo-Yos to create your own unique style of edging trims.

YO-YO TRIMS

1. Experiment with various sizes of circles to achieve your desired effect. Draw the desired size circles on fabric and cut out. Finished yo-yo will be about ½ the diameter of the cut circle.

2. Thread a needle with matching double thread and knot end. Fold over ⅛" to ¼" to the wrong side of the circle. Make a running stitch (see Terms and Tools, page 135), around the outside of the circle. Without breaking the thread, pull gently to form gathers.

3. Continue to pull up gathers and adjust. Turn right side out.

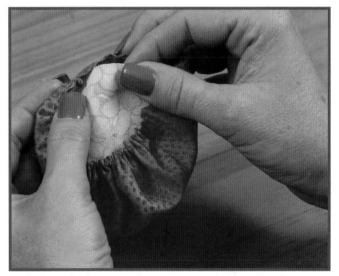

4. If desired, slip a smaller spray-starched circle of contrasting color fabric inside the yo-yo at this time. This "peek-a-boo" yo-yo will resemble a flower.

5. Pull threads together tightly, tie off and clip threads. Finger press the yo-yo flat.

6. Attach yo-yos in desired arrangement to the finished edges of your quilt with small slip stitches (see Terms and Tools, page 135).

Tools & Terms

For quilters, there are numerous specialty tools and terms that make any project fast, fun and done! We've included a Glossary of Terms and assembled a collection of Tools of the Trade which may increase your knowledge of quilting, and prove helpful as you complete your own quilts with beautiful borders, backings, and bindings.

Glossary of Terms

Appliqué: Fabric shapes or motifs that are sewn onto a quilt border fabric for extra dimension or interest. Appliqué can be done by hand or machine.

Hand Appliqué For this method:
- Using template plastic or freezer paper, trace around each appliqué shape and cut out.
- Draw around the template onto right side of desired fabric using pencil, chalk pencil or washable sewing marker.

  - Cut out appliqué ¼" beyond traced line.
  - If multiple layers of appliqué are needed, begin working at the background and work forward.
- Using the drawn line as your guide, slip stitch the appliqué into place. Use your needle to fold under the seam allowance. Take a ⅛" stitch down through the background fabric. Bring the needle up through the fold of the appliqué catching a few threads of the appliqué fabric. Insert the needle as close as possible to where it came up and continue around the appliqué shape.

Machine Appliqué For this method use paper-backed lightweight fusible web, follow the manufacturer's instructions for tracing and fusing:
- Trace the appliqué shape onto the paper side of the fusible web. Cut the fusible web about ⅛" from the outside traced line.

- Fuse the pattern to the wrong side of desired fabric. Cut out on the traced line. Transfer any dashed placement lines to the fabric.

- Peel off the paper backing. Position the appliqué on the background fabric, overlapping the pieces at the dashed lines, if necessary. Fuse in place. Machine stitch using a zig-zag or buttonhole stitch.

Back-to-Front Binding: Binding that is formed by folding the backing layer of the quilt forward over the batting layer and quilt top. The folded edge is then stitched in place.

Backing: Fabric for the back or bottom layer of a quilt. The backing is sometimes referred to as the lining.

Backstitch: Reinforcing the beginning or end of a seam, by going in reverse when machine stitching.

Batting: The thin, soft middle layer that is between the backing and front of a quilt.

Bias Binding: Bias-cut fabric strips used to cover the edges of the top, bottom and batting layers of a quilt.

Bias Grain: The diagonal of the fabric weave. (It stretches.)

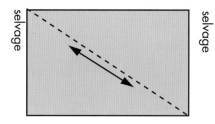

Bias Strips: Narrow strips of fabric cut on the bias grain. Bias is used to form shapes, such as vines and stems in an appliqué border. Wider strips can be used for binding.

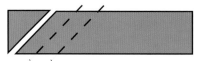

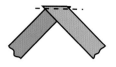

Binding: The technique of finishing the edges of a quilt. The fabric that is used to cover the top, bottom, and batting layers of a quilt.

Blocks: The units that are sewn together to make up the quilt center or border.

Border: The frame or outer edge of a quilt. Can be pieced, appliqué, or plain fabric.

Contrast: The difference between lightness and darkness in fabrics.

Cording: The cord or filler that is sewn inside piping.

Cording Foot: A special sewing machine foot used for stitching close to cording when sewing piping.

Cross-Grain Binding: Cross-Grain fabric strips sewn together and used to cover the edges of the quilt top, batting layer and backing of a quilt.

Crosswise Grain: The threads of fabric that run perpendicular to the selvage. Crosswise grain has slightly more give than lengthwise grain.

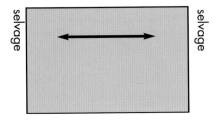

Diagonal: Lines or seams that run at a slant.

Double-Fold Binding: Binding strips that are cut from fabrics and sewn together into one long strip. The strip is then folded lengthwise and pressed. The binding is sewn to the quilt and folded again around the layers of the quilt and stitched in place. Binding strips may be cut from the bias or cross-grain of the fabric.

Edgings: A method for finishing the edges of a quilt other than binding. Effect used for decorative and irregular edges.

Even-Feed or Walking Foot: Sewing machine attachment that feeds the top fabric at the same rate as the bottom fabric. The walking foot is used for machine quilting; also useful for attaching binding.

Freezer Paper: Paper that has a dull paper side and shiny wax or plastic side. Useful for appliqué patterns and planning borders. Available at grocery stores.

Hanging Sleeve: A piece of fabric that allows a quilt to be slipped over a pole for wall display, usually added to the back of the quilt after the quilting has been completed and before the binding is applied. To make a hanging sleeve:
- Cut a strip 8½" wide and 1" shorter than the finished width of the quilt.
- Hem each short end by pressing under a ½" hem and then ½" again. Topstitch the hem in place.
- Press the hanging sleeve in half lengthwise. Pin the strip to the top backside of the quilt, with raw edges even. The raw edges will be covered by the binding. Baste in place with a ¼" seam allowance.
- After the binding is attached and sewn to the quilt, smooth and pin the pressed fold of the hanging sleeve to the back. Slip stitch to the back of the quilt, taking care to only go through the back and batting layers of the quilt.

Horizontal: Lines or seams that run side to side.

Glossary of Terms

Lengthwise Grain: The threads of the fabric that run parallel to the selvage. Lengthwise grain has the least amount of give.

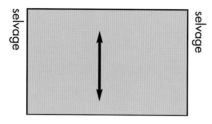

Mitered Corner or Seam: A corner that meets in a 45-degree angle.

Pearl Cotton: An embroidery thread with soft sheen that comes in skeins or on spools and can be used for decorative stitching or quilting.

Piping: A narrow accent of fabric sewn between borders or inside the binding of a quilt. May include cording inserted into a tube of fabric.

Piping Foot: A sewing machine attachment with a slot on the underside that allows it to ride at the top of the piping.

Prairie Points: Pieces of square fabric folded into triangles and sewn to the edges of the quilt.

Quilt Center: The pieced or appliquéd setting of the quilt top that will be surrounded by a border.

Quilt Sandwich: The three layers of a quilt. The quilt top, the middle batting layer and quilt backing.

```
TOP
BATTING
BACKING
```

Right Side of Fabric: The top or printed side of fabric.

Press: Using an iron to crease or fold fabric. When pressing raise the iron up and down. Avoid sliding it back and forth.

Random: Fabrics or quilt pieces that are placed in no particular order.

Quilting:

Hand Quilting For this method:
- Using hand quilting thread; thread a quilting needle with an 18" length of thread. Tie a small knot at the end. Insert the needle through the quilt top and into batting about 1" from where you want to begin quilting. Bring the needle up at the beginning of the quilting line. Give the thread a gentle tug to pull the knot through the quilt top and down into the batting.
- Take several small running stitches at a time, keeping stitches even and as close together as possible (1/8" to 1/4").
- To end a line of stitching, make a small knot close to the fabric. Insert the needle into the fabric and bring it out again about 1" from the end of the stitching. Pop the knot through the quilt top into the batting and clip the thread close to the quilt top.

Machine Quilting Check your sewing machine manual for help with these tips:
- Use a walking foot for straight stitching of quilting lines. This will help to keep all layers of the quilt even. Pivot the fabric by keeping the needle in the down position when changing directions.
- Quilting stencils may be used for all types of designs. The embroidery or darning foot and lowering the feed dogs is helpful for this style of quilting.

Rotary Cutter: A pizza cutter style of tool with a razor sharp blade designed to cut fabric into strips. To be used with a rotary mat. Available at sewing stores.

Rotary Mat: A special surface to use when cutting with a rotary cutter.

Rotary Rulers and Triangles: Measuring tools of plastic or acrylic designed for use with a rotary cutter and rotary mat.

Ruffled Edging: Gathered or pleated strips of fabric sewn to the edges of a quilt or quilt top.

Fabric Scissors: Good sharp scissors for cutting fabric shapes and trimming threads.

Paper Scissors: Good scissors that won't be hurt by cutting paper or template plastic.

Running Basting Stitch:

Sewing Scissors: Good small useful scissors used to clip threads and seams when sewing.

Seam allowance: The distance between the raw edge and the seam line.

Selvage: The finished or lengthwise edge of fabric.

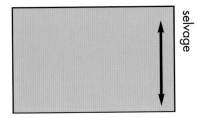

Slip Stitch:

Strip: A width of fabric cut from fabric. Sometimes it will be a specific length.

Strip Piecing: A technique of sewing strips together and then sub-cutting into units. The units are then reassembled into blocks or sections. These can then be used for borders or corners.

Template: A shape or pattern piece for piecing or appliqué.

Template Plastic or Materials: Used to make a shape or template for piecing or appliqué.

Value: The brilliance or lack of brilliance with respect to color of a fabric.

Vertical: Lines or seams that run up and down.

Walking Foot: (See Even-Feed, page 133.)

Wrong Side of Fabric: The side that is not the printed side or top.

Yo-Yo: A circle of fabric that is gathered at the edges. It is then flattened and can be attached to the edges of a quilt. Yo-Yos can also be used as an embellishment on a border.

Zipper Foot: A special sewing machine foot used in sewing zippers and piping. The foot allows for sewing tightly next to cording.

SEWING MACHINE FEET

Sewing machines today have many helpful attachments and feet to make our sewing easier. Some may be included with the purchase of a machine. Your sewing machine dealer will provide attachments for the specific model of your machine.

Walking Feet: Each brand looks slightly different. Some machines have a built in even-feed that works the same way. This attachment is very helpful when applying binding because it feeds the top of the quilt at the same rate as the feed dogs move the bottom of the quilt.

Zipper Feet: When making and sewing piping, the foot rides next to the cording and allows for a tight stitching next to cording. This foot is also used to sew the piping to the quilt.

Double Piping Foot: Pictured upside down, this foot has a groove on the bottom and rides atop the cording when making piping and sewing it to the quilt.

Ruffler: Most sewing manufacturers offer a ruffler. It is helpful when making yards and yards of ruffles. It eliminates the need to sew and pull up gathering.

THREADS, RIBBONS & TRIMS

Today's quilter can choose from a wonderful array of thread. Cotton and cotton-polyester blends are great for almost any quilting purpose, especially piecing and appliqué. Most hand quilters prefer a special hand-quilting thread for stitching layers together. Machine quilters have many choices to add surface interest. You will find lots of variegated threads in quilting weights. Rayon threads have a silky sheen, and pearl cotton makes a bold statement, but it can only be used in the bobbin. When using a decorative weight thread, test it on a sample, and adjust your machine's tension, if necessary. Or, use disappearing .004mm nylon thread for invisible quilting stitches.

Other tools that will help you make beautiful borders, backings, and bindings:
- Fabric marking pencils and fabric markers to help you mark seam allowances, appliqué positions, and quilting lines.
- Silk pins have fine shafts and sharp points to avoid making permanent holes in fabrics.
- Ribbons and braids can be sewn atop a border before or after the quilt is bound.
- Binding clips help hold folded edges when turning binding.
- Hand scissors and thread cutters for snipping threads as you hand or machine sew.
- Quilting needles are helpful for hand quilting and hand stitching many bindings.

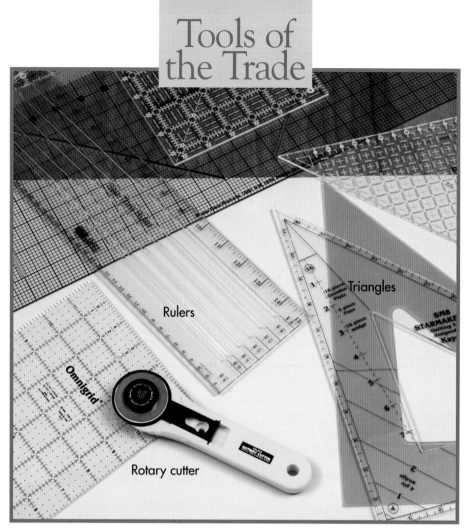

Tools of the Trade

Rulers

Triangles

Rotary cutter

Omnigrid

CUTTING TOOLS

Cutting tools are essential for successful quilting. Many different styles of rulers, triangles, rotary cutters and mats are available for quilting today.

Choose rulers with clear markings and varied widths and lengths. Triangles with or without markings are helpful for mitering.

A rotary mat with a smooth surface and a solid rotary cutter will complete your set of cutting tools.

Freezer paper

Fabric scissors

Paper scissors

Interfacing

Template plastic

TEMPLATE MATERIALS

Template materials are needed for pieced borders with diamonds and irregular shapes as well as appliqué shapes. Template plastic, freezer paper and heavy non-woven interfacing can be helpful to achieve accuracy.

Quilting requires both paper scissors for pattern preparation and precision/sharp-bladed scissors for cutting fabric.

Quilt Sources Gallery

Special thanks to the quilters and quilt collectors for allowing us to share with you the many examples of borders and bindings in our galleries.

Diane Crawford
Cindy Ohmart
Jill Reber

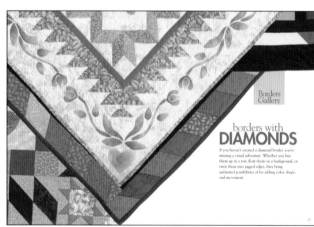

Jill Reber

Diane Crawford
Jill Reber

Diane Crawford
Jill Reber
Margaret Sindelar

Diane Crawford
Cindy Ohmart
Jill Reber
Margaret Sindelar

Diane Crawford
Cindy Ohmart
Jill Reber

Diane Crawford
Jill Reber

Quilt Sources Gallery

Thank you to Pfaff American Sales Corporation and
Husqvarna-Viking Sewing Machines for providing
sewing machines to Jill Reber and Margaret Sindelar
for use in this book.

Jill Reber

Diane Crawford
Cindy Ohmart
Jill Reber
Margaret Sindelar

Diane Crawford
Jill Reber

Jill Reber

Cindy Ohmart
Jill Reber

Jill Reber

Diane Crawford
Cindy Ohmart
Margaret Sindelar